HOW TO
Customize Your
HARLEY-DAVIDSON

Timothy Remus

Motorbooks International
Publishers & Wholesalers ®

First published in 1998 by Motorbooks International Publishers & Wholesalers, 729 Prospect Avenue, PO Box 1, Osceola, WI 54020-0001

The information in this book is true and complete to the best of our knowledge. All recommendations are made without any guarantee on the part of the author or Publisher, who also disclaim any liability incurred in connection with the use of this data or specific details

We recognize that some words, model names and designations, for example, mentioned herein are the property of the trademark holder. We use them for identification purposes only. This is not an official publication

Motorbooks International books are also available at discounts in bulk quantity for industrial or sales-promotional use. For details write to Special Sales Manager at the Publisher's address

Remus, Timothy
How to customize your Harley-Davidson / Timothy Remus.
    p.   cm.
    Includes index.
    ISBN 0-7603-0359-2
(paperback :
    alk. paper)
    1. Harley-Davidson motorcycle—Customizing.
2. Harley-Davidson motorcycle—Customizing—Pictorial works.
I. Title.
TL448.H3R464 1998
629.28'775—dc21   97-43422

Printed in Hong Kong through World Print, Ltd.

On the front cover: State of the Harley customizing art from builder Dave Perewitz. The custom Perewitz frame is graced by Perewitz/Sullivan Brothers billet wheels and the whole machine is done up in a very cool Nancy Brooks graphic design.

On the frontispiece: Though many customizers opt for Evolution-based machines, Shovelheads still offer a popular, though less common, option. This FXR custom is owned by Charlie Anderson.

On the back cover: Top: Wild paint, trick wheels, aftermarket carb, and lots of billet goodies make this eye-catching Softail. Lower left: Custom paint is the hallmark of many hot rod Harleys. Lower right: When too much displacement is just about enough, the aftermarket offers numerous options for the dedicated motorhead. This 140-cubic-inch monster was built at Minneapolis Custom Cycle.

Edited by: Greg Field
Designed by: Amy T. Huberty

CONTENTS

ACKNOWLEDGMENTS 4

INTRODUCTION 5

CHAPTER

1   PLANNING AND DESIGN 6

2   DISASSEMBLY 12

3   FRAMES 16

4   SUSPENSION AND BRAKES 24

5   WHEELS AND TIRES 40

6   EVOLUTION HOP-UP 50

7   AFTERMARKET V-TWINS .86

8   SHEET METAL 96

9   CUSTOM PAINT 114

10 BOLT-ON CUSTOMIZING .134

INDEX 160

ACKNOWLEDGMENTS

This book is considerably bigger than its predecessor, which means there are even more people to thank than last time. For powder-coating sequences I thank Dick White at Best Coat in Blaine, Minnesota. Blaine, a northern suburb of Minneapolis, has become a hot spot for motorcycle and automotive specialty shops to the extent that I've taken to calling the corridor along Highway 65 the "Blaine Special Vehicles Mall."

Next door to Best Coat is M-C Specialties where Mike and the boys always had the welcome mat out when I came by to document the conversion of a Dresser into a Road King. And just up the street is the new home of Donnie Smith Custom Cycles, where Donnie, Rob, Don, and Scott fabricate and assemble some of the nicest custom machines seen anywhere—all while moving bikes and stopping in the middle of projects to accommodate me and my camera.

If you move south along the Highway 65 corridor you find another small cluster of shops. At Metal Fab, Jim and Neil make parts for two and four wheelers, including the occasional scratch-built chain guard for a certain how-to book. Next door is Deters Polishing, where Joe shows us how to take an industrial process and turn it into an art form.

Just a few miles south of Metal Fab and Deters Polishing is Kokesh MC Parts—not in Blaine, technically, but close enough to be included here. I must pass on a big collective "thank you" to Jason, Gary, Gary, Bug, Lee, and Elmer. They always help me with photos, proofread my manuscripts, pass along information learned over many years in the business, and generally save my butt when it most needs saving. And though he's a customer, not an employee, I will take this opportunity to thank Don Hand for the Sportster engine sequences.

Farther south in Minneapolis proper is Minneapolis Custom Cycle. Pat and Greg took time to explain the finer points of scratch building engines and set up a series of photo shoots I needed to round out the book. I must also thank the LaCroix brothers, who own and run Ken's Metal Finishing in north Minneapolis, for at least 10 years of help with my how-to stories.

For providing the dealer perspective and being generally helpful I must express my gratitude to the crew at St. Paul Harley-Davidson. In particular, I owe a debt of thanks to parts-man-extraordinaire George Edwards and hot-rod mechanic Tim Wolff.

Farther south (much farther) in Richmond, Virginia, Lee Clemens runs Departure Bike Works. I need to thank Lee for taking time for a lengthy phone interview and a discussion of the finer points of dyno testing.

Let me finish with a collective thanks to all the aftermarket manufacturers for providing information and photos, to Ken Madden for the great engine illustrations, and to Jaye Strait from Britech for the coating information.

Though she always gets mentioned last it doesn't mean she's any less important than all those Harley guys. The "she" in question is, of course, my lovely and talented wife, Mary Lanz, who cooks when I can't and runs film to the photo lab so these monster projects get turned in on time.

Tim Remus

INTRODUCTION

Time has a way of slipping by and suddenly it seems like centuries ago that Motorbooks International published the first version of *How To Customize Your Harley-Davidson*. Since writing that book, the world of V-Twins has changed more than I could have predicted.

The changes include the phenomenal growth in all things Harley-Davidson, including the number and variety of parts available both from Milwaukee and the aftermarket. Each new group of parts means there are more and more things you can do with that Harley-Davidson in your garage. Not only are there more parts, but there are more models to use as a starting point for that customizing project.

The first book dealt mostly with FXRs, Softails, Shovelheads, and Sportsters. Today we have one totally new family of bikes to customize, the Dyna line. There is also more interest in Dressers, which were only starting to come into their own as objects to be customized at the time the first book was published.

What It Is

Like the first book, this one covers the basics of customizing: planning the project, modifying frames and engines, using the best suspension and brakes, modifying the sheet metal, and painting that sheet metal.

Broader coverage and significantly more detail are the watchwords for this new edition, however. The engine chapter, for example, includes a whole section on aftermarket offerings. Smaller items, like nuts and bolts and spokes, are covered in a series of detailed sidebars. Rather than just provide a chrome plating section, there is information on polishing, powder coating, and even some high-tech coatings that many builders never even consider.

The book covers the full range of modifications from simple how-to projects and easy customizing formulas to elaborate full-custom treatments performed by professional builders. The current Harley-Davidson customizing craze is prone to "one-upmanship." I've tried to keep the emphasis of the book on good design and clever use of parts rather than any insistence that you must buy the newest and the latest. We all have a budget. The idea here is to help you get the most bang for the buck, to create the best-looking, best-running bike you can for a given dollar figure. My hope is that this book will help you determine how to best spend those finite dollars.

As mentioned, this book covers all the current models from Sportsters to Dressers. Likewise the engine sections include information on factory Evos, both Big Twin and Sportster, as well as larger displacement offerings from the aftermarket. There is not, however, much engine information on the pre-Evo engines, both because Evos are the most commonly modified bikes and because I could only cover so much ground.

What It's Not

Despite all the information we've crammed into these pages, you will likely want to go out and buy at least one more book before tearing into that two-wheeled project in the garage. In particular, you should plan to buy a good service manual for the model you're customizing, because extensive though this fine book might be, it doesn't include things like torque specifications and has only limited assembly sequences.

In the end I hope the book helps you toward your goal: to create the best bike you can. A good blend of form and function, a two-wheeled expression of your own ideas. A bike you can point to as being better than new, because anyone can buy a new bike while only a few can build their own.

CHAPTER 1

PLANNING AND DESIGN

Contents

First Things First 6

Deciding How Far to Go 7

Keep it Legal 8

Designing Your Bike 8

A Matter of Style 8

Stay Focused 11

This is perhaps the hardest chapter to write, because it's not about specific procedures or hard parts. This chapter is about making the best decisions early in the project so the bike you end up with is both good looking and useful.

There are some make-or-break decisions that have a major impact on the amount of time and money you spend on this project. If you understand the importance of the decisions, you are more likely to take the time to think each one through.

And though it seems the fancy bikes with lots of expensive parts get all the attention in the magazines, there are plenty of killer machines built on a budget. If you want good visual impact, plan the bike carefully. Understand that each part affects and is affected by all the others. Don't just say, "I'm going to paint it black [or green or whatever] because I like black bikes." The paint job you choose is probably the most important single decision you will make regarding the overall look of the bike.

Throughout this chapter I've tried to illustrate good design ideas—as seen through my jaded perspective—with example bikes. These may or may not be expensive. They may or may not be show winners. But I think they all illustrate good design. These example bikes cover a lot of ground, both in terms of money spent and in the type of bike they represent. Ultimately, they are intended to highlight clever ideas and to make you

think. And the more you think about this bike-building project and the more you plan, the more likely you are to succeed.

First Things First

Before you start to lay out detailed plans for the new customized motorcycle, you've got to be honest with yourself. You need to ask the following questions: How much money do you have to spend, how much of the work can you really do yourself, and what is the timeline for the new bike—when does it need to be finished?

Lying to yourself about the budget will only result in a bike that doesn't get finished because you don't have the cash to finish it. Or a bike that turns out half-assed because you had to skimp on materials at the end of the project. Closely related to the money issue is the matter of time and skill. If you don't have any free time you're going to have to pay other people to build and assemble the bike. Most of us farm out some of the work; how much we send out to other people depends not just on available free time but on our own mechanical skills as well.

Allowing yourself enough time for the project will ensure that you don't have to stay up all night to get it finished before the show. Extra time will also allow for delays that always seem to occur when you're dealing with an outside labor source like the painter or plating shop. Remember that painters and platers have busy periods and slack periods

This very bright Softail features loud pipes and an even louder paint job. Note the painted frame, wild graphics, and abundant use of billet aluminum, including the Performance Machine wheels and four-piston calipers.

the bike stripped bare you can rake and mold the frame and then paint it any color you want. Because you have the engine out of the frame you can do as much work on the internals or externals as your budget allows. This is not to say that all of us should start fixing up the old FXR by taking out every bolt we can find.

Understand that though stripping the bike to the frame might provide a certain freedom in the things that can be done to the bike, it also means the project will be much more expensive and time consuming.

Don't assume the engine must come out of the frame before the bike can be customized. You can change the sheet metal, wheels, and suspension—all without stripping the bike to its birthday suit. With

determined by the season and the date of the next big run. Avoid asking the polishing shop to completely polish the primary cover and rocker boxes in two days—when it's only two weeks until Sturgis.

This book assumes that the majority of readers are starting with a complete or mostly complete Harley-Davidson motorcycle. At the extremes, the process of customizing your bike can be as simple as a paint job or as complex as a compete disassembly and rebuild.

Deciding How Far to Go

Part of this planning process involves deciding how far to go with the project. Do you intend to keep it simple with fresh paint on stock sheet metal or do you intend to pull the bike down to a bare frame and start over?

There is a major dividing line that separates the simple repaint from the complex customization, and that is whether or not you take the engine out of the frame. With

Compare this Softail to the bright orange beauty seen above. The two bikes are examples of the very different, yet pleasing, things that can be done with the same chassis. This bike uses spoked, 16-inch wheels and tail-dragger type fenders to achieve a more classic look.

KEEP IT LEGAL

Though most of this book is concerned with customizing Harley-Davidson motorcycles that already exist and already have a clear title, some readers will want to build either a complete bike or a complete engine from aftermarket parts. Before proceeding, take a minute to read and consider the following legal considerations—they may save you a great deal of time and money.

Before providing a title for a scratch-built bike, most states will require that you provide an MSO (manufacturers statement of origin) with serial numbers for both the engine cases and the frame. When you buy a frame, engine cases, or a complete engine from any legitimate aftermarket supplier you will get an MSO. Be sure it is filled out correctly and that any previous transfers are noted. If the paperwork isn't clean, don't buy the parts.

A complete used engine might not be such a hot deal, unless you buy it from a reputable dealer or junkyard that can provide the necessary paperwork. It goes without saying (but I'll say it anyway) that all the paperwork must be completed to the satisfaction of your state licensing authority.

For the same reason, it's not a good idea to base your new engine on a set of used Harley-Davidson cases. Without an MSO, the state will not give you a title for the new bike. If you're putting a complete aftermarket engine in an already completed and licensed motorcycle, you need to take the title for the bike and the MSO for the new engine to the state so the new engine can be noted on the title. You may also be required to bring the bike to the state motor vehicle testing station for an inspection.

You must keep the receipts for everything you buy for the new scratch-built bike and/or engine. In this way you can prove to the state that the parts are not stolen and also that the sales tax has already been paid. Sometimes people buy a set of new aftermarket engine cases and then a complete engine, minus cases, at the swap meet. Then they install the swap meet internals into the new, legal, cases. The result is a cheap, legal engine. Life is good until it comes time to prove to the state that you bought everything, including the pistons, flywheel assembly, cylinders, and so on. Even if the state doesn't give you a hard time, it doesn't make good sense to support the people who might steal *your* new bike.

The professional shops all recommend that you keep perfect records and paperwork during the project. A photo record, to back up the paperwork, is a good idea, too. That way you will be able to get a nice clean title with minimal hassles from the state authorities.

only a change in sheet metal, and the right accessories and hardware to accent the sheet metal, some very tasty custom bikes can be built.

What you can't do, however, without pulling the bike all the way down to the bare essentials, is paint or mold the frame. This means you must stay with the black frame and that you must choose a color scheme for the sheet metal that will work with a black frame.

Making this decision as to whether or not to pull the bike down to the frame is affected by your earlier budget and time considerations. Painting and molding the frame means the project will be two or three times as much work than it would be if all you did was to paint or change the sheet metal and add some accessories. So before deciding to "go all the way," think seriously about the time and dollars you can set aside for this particular project.

Designing Your Bike

Before you can design your new bike you have to determine how the bike will be used. Big stroker motors sound great and make gobs of torque but may not have the longevity of a mildly souped-up 80 cubic inch V-Twin.

Is this going to be your only bike? Do you want to ride it from Boston to Sturgis? Maybe you already own a nice dresser and this new machine is intended to be the proverbial bar-hopper.

A Matter of Style

After you've been brutally honest with yourself about how

A great Jon Kosmoski paint job with reverse flames, combined with tasteful accessories makes for a good looking Dyna. This bike looks good without a painted frame or aftermarket brakes. Even the factory air cleaner was used—after being painted to match the rest of the bike.

you're going to use the bike and how much money you can spend, you need to consider style. What exactly do you want this machine to look like? Is nostalgia your goal, or is the bike you want something more modern with bright, skateboard neon graphics?

Before starting on a customer bike, most professional bike builders send the customer home with a stack of magazines and orders to, "mark all the bikes you really like." In a similar fashion, you should have your own photo file of favorite bikes. Eventually, you need a picture or detailed sketch of what you want the new bike to look like, especially if you're stripping the bike to the frame and starting over. Though it might be tempting to just pull the bike apart without a real plan, it's dangerous to just "let it happen." The plans and sketches should be detailed—you

don't need a $10,000 surprise.

Experienced builders often start with a photo of a bike similar to the one they want to build. They make big black and white blow-ups of the photo at the local copy and printing store. Now they can "customize" the bike with scissors and glue. A different fork rake is just a matter of cutting and pasting. A new color can be had simply by purchasing some colored markers. Cut, paste and then make more copies. This is a cheap way to visualize and finalize your plans for the new bike.

The more elaborate (and expensive) your plan, the more important it is to take the time to work through some design exercises. You can hire an artist to do a color rendering of the new bike. In this way you get to see your ideas as seen through the artist's eye. Arlen Ness often starts with a photo of the

rolling chassis and then lays tracing paper over the photo. Sketches of the new bike are done on the tracing paper. This way the new body panels or gas tank are superimposed on the rolling chassis—so they're sure to fit the bike and stay in proportion to the actual chassis.

Whether you use a simple sketch or a sophisticated rendering, it's important to know ahead of time what the bike will look like. Keep the image of the new bike taped to the toolbox; it will keep you focused on the project and prevent your being distracted when a new fad blows into town.

Most professional builders mock up the bike before the paint is applied. They set the frame on the hoist or workbench and clamp or bolt on the fenders, tank(s), and wheels. You need to know that all the parts fit the bike and that all

Hardtails are making a big comeback. This scalloped ride combines early styling cues with modern billet triple trees, brakes, and accessories. Just to prove that not all the cool bikes are built in big shops by professionals, Jeff Guedes of Brooklyn Park, Minnesota, built this bike at home in his spare time and did all the work, including the paint job and even the pinstriping.

the holes line up. This is a good time to look over the bike to ensure that the parts fit in a design or aesthetic sense. To get a proper look at the bike it should be up off the floor in a shop that's big enough so you can actually step back to really "see" the bike the way it's going to look on the street. Some builders roll the mock-up outside and then look it over from various angles.

Sometimes a slight change in the position or angle of a fender makes a tremendous difference in the way a machine looks. The mock-up stage is a good time to double-check the good looks of your new design. This is the time to see how a different fender looks on the bike, or how the lines of the tank work with the overall design.

Money, usage, and style are the three things that will deter-mine the type of bike you build. Seldom do all three categories agree. When conflicts arise you need to decide which parts of your new design are the most important. The new billet wheels are great, but for the price of two wheels you can pay for the paint job, or sheet metal, or a pair of aftermarket cylinder heads. Work through the give-and-take until you've designed a

Built by Donnie Smith for a special friend, this Sportster gets its great looks from the additional rake and the bright orange-to-black paint job with flames. Gas tank is from an FXR; small air dam is from Chrome Specialties.

Though out of production for a few years now, the FXR chassis is still used by customizers like Dave Perewitz to build some great looking bikes. Note the stretched, raked frame with the new front section and integral rear fender struts. Gas tanks are stretched to match and painted with an elaborate flag graphic by Nancy Brooks. Wheels are new Perewitz designs measuring 19 inches for the front and 16 inches for the back.

bike you can enjoy and be proud to call your own.

Once you get into the project, try to keep realistic goals. This all sounds too simple, but be sure to set aside enough time to do each job and do it right. Doing it right starts during the disassembly stage. This machine is going to be a pile of parts for some time and you're unlikely to remember where each bolt went when it comes time for the reassembly. Make the job of putting it all back together easier by grouping parts and bolts into separate boxes or shelves in the shop. Small groups of bolts can be put in Ziploc bags with a label. If all this sounds trite, consider that the time you don't spend looking for missing bolts can be spent assembling the bike—or working extra hours at the job so

you can pay for the new bike.

Speaking of time, try to get something done every week so the bike doesn't sit so long that you lose your momentum. And remember that outside work like paint and upholstery always takes longer than the original estimate; it's all part of Murphy's law.

Stay Focused

So you must take a realistic look at how much money you're going to spend. Of that money, you need to decide how much will be spent on outside labor. What you need is a budget. An honest-to-God list of each major part and its cost. Then a separate series of items, one for each outside labor operation—paint, powder coating, possible upholstery. Enter each item and its cost. Be real-

istic on the cost. Don't forget the "miscellaneous" category for all the little things that don't have categories of their own. Things like the chrome Allen bolts you want to use throughout the bike and the billet mirrors from the Arlen Ness or Custom Chrome catalog.

Once the bike is past the mock-up stage, avoid the temptation to change its style. New fads come and go, but you need to finish the current project. If you start second-guessing the design halfway through the project, you'll never get finished. Stick with your original design and work it through to completion.

The rewards are great but it ain't easy or cheap. So plan carefully: be sure you've got enough money (or almost enough) and time to do it the right way the first time.

Contents

Be Neat 12

How Far Is Too Far? 13

Nuts and Bolts 14

Now Is the Time 15

Disassembly may seem like the simplest thing in the world. After all, who needs any help tearing everything apart? In just one Saturday afternoon, you and a friend can have that bike completely ripped apart. Six or eight hours after starting you can look with satisfaction at the bare frame, the engine in one corner, a pile of fenders and wheels in another. The trouble comes two or six months later when you start to reassemble the bike. Suddenly you have no idea which bolts (from among all those bolts) hold on the front calipers. Worse, you may spend all your time looking for the brake hoses or the small crush washers that seal the hose to the caliper—instead of spending your time building the motorcycle.

Disassembly may seem to be the easiest part of the task. Builders should remember, however, that *how* the bike is disassembled will determine how easy it is to reassemble. By being neat and thinking ahead, you can make the reassembly a pleasant task rather than an enormous headache.

Be Neat

When you tear apart that Harley in the garage, take a minute first to find some boxes and a marker pen. As the fenders and large chunks come off the bike, put them in boxes and label each box. Organize the boxes in logical order. One might be labeled, "front fork," while another would be, "rear suspension." Small parts,

At one professional shop where they build bikes from scratch, everything that goes with one bike is placed on the shelf with the customer's name on it. Parts are left in their packaging until installation time so nothing gets lost.

nuts and bolts, washers, and screws should go in Ziploc bags and then be placed in the correct box with the rest of the fenders or fork parts or whatever. When the disassembly is finished, put the boxes on the shelf so they don't get lost or kicked across the garage floor.

This way, there is no question as to which bolts were used for the calipers. When the time comes you can spend your time putting your new bike together, not looking for misplaced parts or wondering which bolt fits which hole.

Small plastic bins make it easy to group parts as they come off the bike.

How Far Is Too Far?

The time has come to take the bike apart. You've waited all summer for this. Finally, one Saturday morning when it's too cool to ride, you and a buddy start into disassembly with enthusiasm. When the question arises—How far are you going to take the bike apart?—you decide to take it, "all the way down to the frame." That way you figure you can get everything done right. You can paint the frame, you can "rewire" the bike, you can smooth out some of those ugly welds. There seem to be so many good reasons for taking the disassembly process all the way to its final conclusion.

This is one of those situations where the common logic is flawed. Taking the bike all the way down to the frame may be a good idea if

you are sure you're going to mold and/or paint the frame, if you want to modify the frame, or if the bike has a lot of miles on it and truly needs a complete going through.

Too many people rip the bike apart without a really good idea of what they're doing or what the final goals for the project are. Many of the "basket cases" advertised for sale in the Sunday paper are these misguided projects—projects that were easier to rip apart than they were to correctly reassemble. Remember, taking it apart is always easier than putting it all back together.

So stick with your plan. If you are building a mild custom based on a late-model FXR, there's really no need to rip everything apart. If your plan includes repainting the

fenders, tank, and side covers, take those off, but leave the rest of the bike intact. If you intend to leave the frame black, settle for a good cleaning and a little touch-up where the paint is chipped.

Pulling out that big factory wiring harness in favor of a "simpler" one built at home may not be such a good idea, either. If the harness has rubbed through in a couple of places, just repair those areas. Be sure to solder and carefully tape any repairs you make. Though a lot of those wires seem unnecessary, the Harley engineers just may know more about wiring and electrical systems than you do. Mickey Mouse repair of an otherwise good wiring harness is a sure way to screw up the reliability of your motorcycle.

NUTS AND BOLTS

Complete books have been written on nuts and bolts; what follows is a short introduction to the science of bolting things together.

First, the obvious: Buy good bolts from a quality shop or a good industrial supply house.

Second: Bolts are graded. The best are grade 8, followed by grade 5, and then grade 3 or hardware-store grade. The best bolts are made from forged material and feature rolled threads. Cheap bolts are made from non-forged steel and have threads that are formed by cutting or smashing.

Third: In a given size, a fine-threaded bolt is stronger than a coarse-threaded bolt. This is because the fine-thread bolt has a larger root diameter (the diameter at the base of the threads) and there is more contact between the threads.

Fourth: Allen bolts are nearly always grade 8; it's simply a standard set by the manufacturers.

Fifth: Chrome plating a bolt weakens the bolt slightly, but the bolts they plate are nearly always at least grade 5, and often grade 8. Also, the bolts used by Harley-Davidson to hold its bikes together are generally larger than necessary so there is an "overkill" factor.

Sixth: Chrome bolts may be slightly oversize due to the buildup of material on the threads. The possible oversize means they can gall in the hole. The fact that they're grade 5 or 8 means they're hard as hell to get out if you break one in a blind hole. This means you should chase male and female threads with a tap and die. Also, be sure to use either anti-seize or Loctite on the threads because either one will minimize metal-to-metal contact between male and female threads. With chrome Allen bolts there is seldom any actual plating down in the bottom of the hexagonal recess. The only way to avoid rust forming down in the hole is to apply a little paint to the bottom of the hole, use a chrome cap, or put a little clear silicone on the end of the Allen wrench the first time you use the bolt.

Seventh: Stainless bolts are pretty but not very strong. Even though stainless is tough, it doesn't make strong bolts. Also note, the grading system is different: A grade 8 stainless bolt is equal to only about a grade 3 steel bolt. Stainless bolts tend to stretch and distort more than steel as they are tightened, for this reason they should be used only once and some kind of thread lubricant or anti-seize is a good idea.

Eighth: There are counterfeit bolts around advertised as grade 8 or "better than grade 8." They're not even as good as grade 8. When in doubt refer back to rule number one.

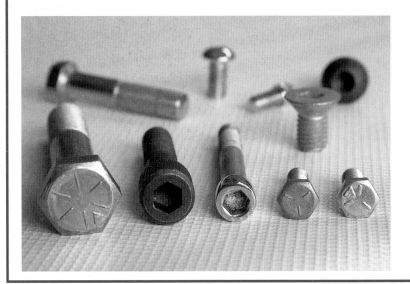

Left to right, a variety of bolts you will find useful. Six slash marks make a grade-8 bolt, next to that are two Allen head bolts (which are nearly always grade 8), on the far right are two grade-5 bolts designated by three slash marks.

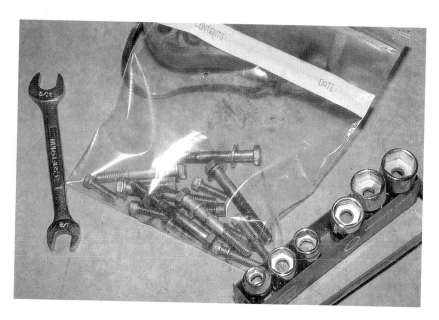

Plastic makes it easy to see exactly what you've got in the bag—a small label can be slipped inside the bag or stuck on the outside.

Once the disassembly is finished, it's a good time to take a good look at the total project. The list of parts to be ordered should be double-checked. Parts that must go to the frame or chrome shop can be set aside, ready to drop off or ship out.

Be sure to allow enough time for the bottlenecks that occur in most projects. Painters and chrome shops don't always work as quickly as most of us would like. Don't make the mistake of letting the swingarm you need chrome-plated sit in your garage for two months before rushing it to the chrome shop pleading for them to turn it around in one week.

With the bike disassembled and cleaned, the project has taken one giant step forward. After a short break to check on the master plan you can actually begin ordering parts and paint. Finally, after spending about twice the time and money you planned, it's time for the best part of the whole project—bolting the new bike together.

Now Is the Time

There is something that should be done just after disassembly, and that is a good cleaning. There's never going to be a better time to clean that frame or those engine cases or the hidden part of the swingarm. So buy a can of Gunk or some kind of cleaner intended for the job and start scrubbing. A very small wire brush or an old toothbrush will help here. When you've got the big chunks off, start in with some strong soap and water to finish the job. Don't use gasoline or a flammable solvent for cleaning, no matter how convenient it seems at the time.

This is a good time to take an inventory of any worn-out parts that were discovered during the disassembly. Things like worn brake pads (if you're going to keep the factory brakes), cracked brackets, and stripped and missing nuts. Make a list of these items you need and add it to the list of goodies you intend to buy for that "new" motorcycle. And even though you might not be pulling the bike down to the bare frame, it's a good time to repair and clean up parts that attach to the frame. If the swingarm or the brackets that hold the bags are beat up and devoid of paint, send them out for paint or powder paint; there will never be a better time.

If the bike is going to be apart for months while parts are painted and plated, take extra time to sort and label things very carefully. The time you take doing this will pay big dividends when it's time to put Humpty Dumpty back together again.

Contents

Hardtail or Soft? 17

Hardtail 17

Softail 18

Twin-Shock 19

How to Choose
the Right One 19

Frame Modifications 21

Additional Rake 21

Additional Stretch 21

Molding a Frame 22

Painting and Molding
the Frame 24

Rounding It Up 25

The frame of your motorcycle is like the foundation of your house. It is the one thing everything else is built upon. As delivered from the factory, the frame on your Harley-Davidson is extremely strong and sturdy. There's a lot of engineering and overengineering in that factory frame. Don't make poorly conceived and executed modifications to the frame that compromise the product Harley-Davidson worked so hard to build. Any changes made to the frame must be done by qualified personnel so your chassis remains true. All welds must be of the highest quality.

Before discussing your frame options, we need to define terms. "Rake" is the angle of the fork assembly when compared to vertical. Some builders talk about a frame being "raked five degrees." What they mean is that it has five additional degrees of rake. The term "stretch" is most commonly used to describe the amount of material added to the frame, between the seat and the neck. A frame that's stretched three inches is three inches longer between the seat and the neck. Though some builders add material to the front down tubes, we will use "stretch" to describe the dimension between the seat and the neck.

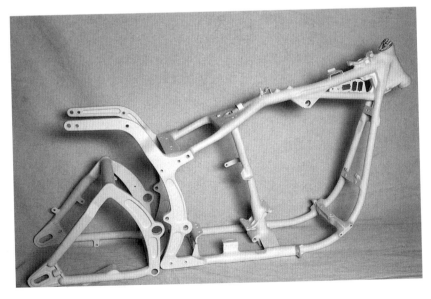

This is a stock Softail frame with just a little extra rake. Note the fender rails integral with the frame, the webbing under the top tube where the factory wiring plugs snap into place, and the pads where the engine and transmission bolt directly to the frame.

Hardtail or Soft?

Whether your frame is from Harley-Davidson or one of the aftermarket companies, there are three basic styles with a large number of variations. Your basic consideration are hardtail, Softail (with the shocks hidden under the chassis), or a twin-shock frame (sometimes called FXR or Dyna style).

Hardtail

A hardtail frame makes a nice basis for a strictly business kind of hot-rod machine. By eliminating the rear suspension the frame is made simpler and less expensive. Hardtail frames have those great lines, the look of a classic V-twin. The downside is the proverbial pounding your backside will take on any extended rides.

This is a modified FXR chassis as seen in Donnie Smith's shop. Note the signature triangular area under the seat and the decidedly non-stock front section that provides both extra stretch and rake.

Not all hardtail frames are the same. This Panhead replacement frame from Moon Machine in Cedar, Minnesota, is a near-clone to the factory frames of the period.

On an FXR, the engine and transmission are bolted together into one assembly that is supported at three points (rubber mounted). Many of the twin-shock aftermarket frames use this same system for mounting the engine.

Though you might think a hardtail is a hardtail, there are a number of interesting alternatives for builders seeking these simplest of frame designs. In addition to rake angles, you can buy your hardtail frame "stretched" (made longer between the seat and the neck) or with stretched lower legs, which raises the neck and provides a much different look.

Some hardtails come with a "wishbone" shape in the front down tubes, and some provide for rubber-mounted engines. Most of the modern hardtails will accept any Big Twin engine, but many are designed for the four-speed transmission. New designs with wider rear sections allow you to use fat rear tires with belt drive.

Softail

By hiding the shocks under the frame, a Softail-style frame provides the look of a hardtail without the harsh ride. The Softail frame, whether from Milwaukee or the aftermarket, can be the basis for some very good-looking custom bikes, with lines and simplicity unmatched by twin-shock frames. Some riders think a Softail frame is the only one to have and the only way to build a bike that truly has "the look." Bikes that feature elaborate body work are often based on Softail frames because, by eliminating the shocks from their traditional location, it is much easier to wrap body work around the rear wheel and the area under the seat.

Yet there is always a cost, and for all the styling advantages of a Softail-style frame there is a penalty. First, the Softail design allows for only about three inches of suspension travel, meaning the ride will never match that of twin-shock bikes with about five inches of travel (this situation gets even worse if you lower the bike, further reducing the suspension travel). Second, most Softail frames mount the engine solid to the frame, meaning the full vibratory ability of that V-twin will be fed to the frame and, ultimately, to you, the rider. Third, though it's a somewhat subjective impression, many riders who have ridden both styles of bikes feel a twin-shock frame handles and rides better than the Softail design.

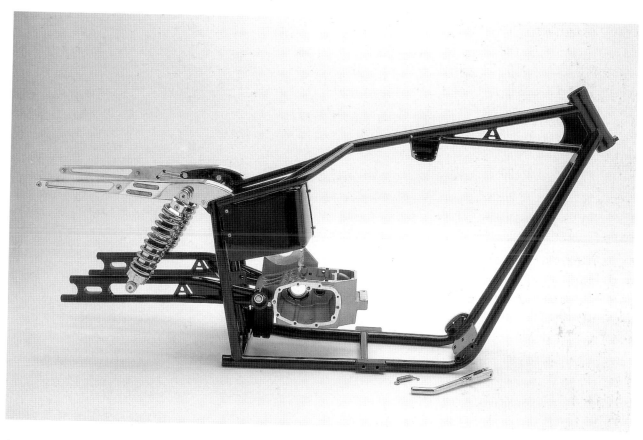

Among the new frame offerings on the market is this rubber-mount twin shock frame from Arlen Ness. This new piece uses a Dyna-style engine mounting system in a frame built from 1-1/4-inch cold rolled tubing. The frame comes with bearing cups and has an integral fork stop. Available with 2- or 5-inch stretch and 35-degree rake. *Arlen Ness Inc.*

Most Softail frames from the aftermarket will accept any Big Twin engine equipped with either a four- or five-speed transmission. Some of the newer designs are just a little taller than the factory frames, meaning they will accept a stroker engine with ease. Many of these frames can be ordered with a wider swingarm and provisions for a wide rear tire and belt drive.

Twin-Shock

Twin-shock frames have been manufactured since the dawn of suspended time. This is a tried and true design providing plenty of suspension travel and (generally) good road manners. The twin-shock frame makes it easy to adjust

the ride height up or down by installing longer or shorter shock absorbers. And though most Softail frames mount the motor to the frame in a solid fashion, most twin-shock frames are "rubber-mounted." By suspending the engine and transmission in rubber, the vibes of the big thumping V-twin are isolated from the rider for a smoother ride and minimal fatigue after a long ride.

The disadvantages of this design include the look, which some riders just don't care for, and the fact that the shocks make it tough to wrap custom sheet metal around the back of the bike.

Though for many years there were only a few of these designs to choose from in the aftermar-

ket, today every major catalog has at least one new twin-shock frame available in a number of configurations.

Most of these frames will accept any Big Twin engine and many will take either a four- or five-speed transmission. Like the modern Softail frames, most manufacturers of twin-shock frames offer a wide-tire kit to accommodate the popular fat-tire look.

How to Choose the Right One

The frame decision will affect and be affected by your choice of an engine, your feelings on style, and the way you will use the bike. First, you need to decide where you want the shocks, or if there should be any shocks at all. Once you've decided on the basic frame type, you need to find the individual frame that's right for your project. Before buying an aftermarket frame you need to talk to some builders and shops in your area, because the quality of aftermarket frames ranges from very good to very bad. The people who know good from bad are the ones building bikes day in and day out.

On the Softail side of the market, the frames break down into OEM (original equipment manufacturer) and non-OEM configurations. The OEM designs come from Harley-Davidson or closely mimic those designs. These frames use factory dimensions and mounting points for tanks and sheet metal. Many OEM-style aftermarket frames go so far as to include the webbing under the top tube so the terminal blocks on the factory wiring harness will snap into place.

The OEM-style frame is nearly always the less-expensive option. Not only are these frames less expensive to buy, they are generally less expensive to equip as well. The frame will accept stock hardware and sheet metal, which tends to be the least expensive. What might be called custom frames with additional stretch require that you use a stretched tank(s) as well. Provisions for extra-wide rear tires mean you must also use a matching extra-wide fender.

Remember that some of the non-OEM or "custom" frames are fairly raw and have no webbing to plug the wiring harness into and no mounting bosses for the Fat Bob tanks. This translates into more work and/or money.

On the twin-shock side of the market, there are stock Harley-Davidson frames and various twin-shock frames from a variety of manufacturers. There are also a few aftermarket frames that mimic the look and dimensions of a Harley-Davidson frame.

Rather than use a duplicate of the factory frame, most manufacturers on this side of the market build their own variation on the twin-shock theme. Among the more popular are the new Pro Street frames from Kenny Boyce and the always popular offerings from Ness. Yes, a true OEM-style frame would probably be cheaper, but very few builders seem to choose that route. In picking a

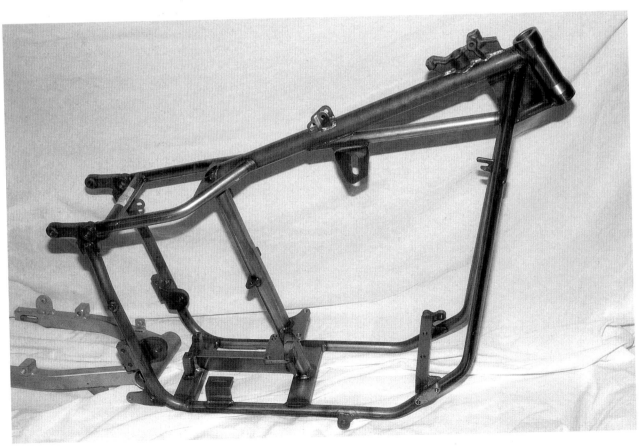

Among the many aftermarket frames available are these solid-mount swingarm frames from CCI. Similar to the old FX factory frames, these are ready for Fat Bob tanks and come with 33-degree fork angles and 2 inches of stretch in the lower legs. Bolt in any Big Twin engine and run belt or chain final drive.

frame of this style you need to find a design that fits your goals for the bike. From short and stubby to long and sleek, there are plenty of these frames out there to chose from.

Before deciding whether to buy a new aftermarket frame and start building from scratch, or to modify an existing Harley-Davidson, consider the following:

1. Your aftermarket bike will be titled according to the frame manufacturer, not as a Harley-Davidson. This may impact the value of the bike and the ease with which you can buy insurance.

2. Many states give a scratch-built bike a "reconstructed title" the same as a bike that was rebuilt from a wreck. Again, this may affect the value and insurability.

3. Building a bike from scratch based on an aftermarket frame allows you a great deal more freedom in what you build, though it also involves more work.

4. Starting from an aftermarket frame makes more sense if you want a radical custom—and the alternative is to buy a late-model Harley-Davidson and then rip it apart and start all over.

Frame Modifications

Rake and stretch are the two most common modifications made to Harley-Davidson motorcycles. The trend is to longer machines with additional rake, and often stretch as well. Though a change in the angle of the fork won't require an additional change, a change in the stretch will require a stretched tank(s) to match.

Additional Rake

Before changing the factory fork angle two questions must be answered: By whom and by how much? As already stated, the shop that does the rake job must be qualified. The end result must be

straight and it must be strong. The question then becomes, "how much?" The rake on stock Harley-Davidson frames runs from about 30 degrees on basic Dyna models, all the way to 32 or 33 degrees on the Softail Customs. Builders like Donnie Smith and Dave Perewitz often run bikes with rake angles of 35 to nearly 40 degrees.

Many builders feel that increasing the rake (effectively kicking the front wheel forward) gives the bike "the look." In this case, "the look" is defined as the long, stretched-out profile—a bike that looks like it's moving when it's standing still. Donnie Smith says it "gives the bike an attitude."

A few problems—all of them serious trade-offs—crop up when the rake is increased past the factory specifications. First, when the fork angle is extended too far the forks become too horizontal and simply don't want to slide up and down any more. Second, increased fork angle gives good straight-line stability, but once the front wheel moves from the straight-ahead position the bars get heavy and the bike wants to "fall into" the turn. Riders talk about "flop" or the tendency of the front wheel to fall against the fork stops during low-speed maneuvers in town.

If more rake is what you've just got to have, then have it in moderation. If possible, ride a bike with some extra rake so you understand first-hand what the trade-offs are and how the machine handles in day-to-day situations.

The work itself must be done by an experienced shop. With an FXR or Dyna-type frame made up of a large box-section near the neck, many shops carefully cut through most of the metal attaching the steering head to the frame. With the use of a jig to keep the steering head straight relative to the rest of the frame, the steering head is pulled away from the rest of the frame at

the bottom (it is still attached at the top) and a small piece of metal (sometimes called a wedge or wedge-rake) is welded into the void.

Additional Stretch

Stretching the frame means adding material to the top tube, but in the real world most builders construct a new front-frame section. These builders commonly convert the box-section tubing that runs from the neck back into a pair of tubes that extend back to meet the factory frame under the gas tank. By replacing the box-section, the front of the frame takes on a much more sculptured look. Gone is the utilitarian look of the factory frame, replaced by the more graceful lines of the replacement tubing.

Because the neck is moved forward, the down tubes must be carefully cut, heated and then bent forward to meet the neck at its new location. Most stock top tubes run uphill slightly, so stretching the frame proves an opportunity to either allow the new section to run farther uphill, or make the new top tube more horizontal. The majority of current builders bring the top tube down during the stretching process to help create the low, rakish profile. On the other hand, there are shops and bike builders who prefer the look of a frame with longer down tubes and a raised neck.

When modifying frames, builders nearly always use the factory neck, because the neck contains the VIN or serial numbers for the bike. Which means it's a good idea to protect those numbers as the frame is raked, molded, and painted. Many builders and painters carefully cut a thin piece of duct tape and cover the numbers before they start welding, grinding, and molding the frame.

Though perhaps not a true frame modification, there exists the possibility of extending the swingarm to stretch the bike's

MOLDING A FRAME

The one thing that truly separates a mild custom from a full custom is the frame—specifically the molded frame on what's commonly called a full-custom motorcycle. Here we document the molding of a modified FXR frame in the small shop of Greg Smith, brother to well-known customizer Donnie Smith. Greg does the work in the evening after working full time in a commercial body shop. Doing the molding over a series of evenings may be an advantage. The forced one- and two-day breaks help relieve the tedium of sanding and more sanding,

and also give the body filler plenty of time to fully cure.

The idea is to smooth out all the welds and metal work, whether they were done by the factory or the fabricator. When molding a frame it's important to avoid grinding into the welds themselves because they're what hold the bike together. The other thing to keep in mind is the importance of keeping the VIN numbers on the neck legible throughout the process. After that it's a matter of having an eye for sculpture and plenty of patience.

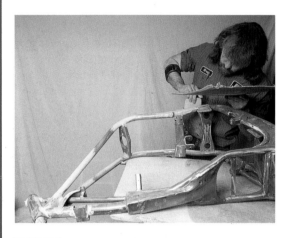

1 Here we see a much-modified FXR frame early in the molding process. Greg Smith started at the neck and is working his way along the frame. Before starting the molding, the frame was sand blasted and all areas that would be molded were roughed up with a 36-grit pad on a small grinder (using great care not to cut into the welds themselves).

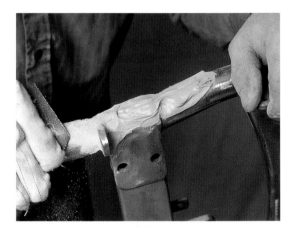

2 Close up shows Smith's material of choice: lightweight, stain-free body filler. Smith recommends using only as much catalyst as the manufacturer recommends, and to mix the two parts thoroughly. Smith uses the filler to sculpt soft curves and radiused corners where ugly welds once lived. Smith puts on the filler in layers, never putting on more than he thinks he needs. Here you can see an area that was already sanded and next to it an area covered with fresh filler. Smith likes to start the sanding—with 36 grit in this case—before the filler is fully hard as this saves a tremendous amount of time.

3 Here, Smith starts in on the large paneled area under the seat. After two or three layers, the filler may be pretty thick, but Smith never worries that it might be too thick and he's never had a problem. The first coat goes down over bare steel sanded with 36 grit; additional coats should go down on filler that's been sanded and then blown off so there is no dust to inhibit adhesion of the next coat

4 The area under the seat is sanded with a 36-grit pad. Nearly all the sanding on a frame must be done by hand. For tight corners Smith sometimes wraps a small wood dowel with sand paper. Small imperfections and pinholes are often filled with two-part glazing compound.

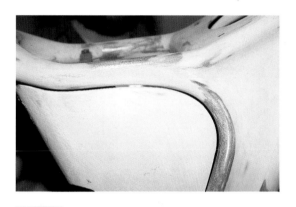

6 After all the pinholes in the filler have been filled with glazing putty and all the molded areas have been sanded with 80-grit paper, Smith applies three heavy coats of primer-surfacer (EP-2 from House of Kolor in this case). This material will easily fill the 80-grit scratches. The gun is a gravity feed HVLP unit. After allowing these first coats to dry for the recommended period of time, he will sand with 120 grit. The next steps are to apply three more coats, allow those to dry, sand with 180 grit, and then apply the final three coats. Smith likes to let the painter do the final sanding before application of the sealer or base coat.

5 The filler (or mud) is used to ensure everything fits perfectly, like the edge of the oil tank where it meets the frame. This requires many trial fittings with applications of filler to low areas and then more sanding, sanding, sanding.

7 The finished frame, ready for one more sanding and then the application of the final paint. Before jumping into your first molding job consider that Smith has about 40 hours of labor invested in this frame

wheelbase. This is another job that requires a jig, a heli-arc welder, and a skilled fabricator. Sportsters in particular benefit from a longer swingarm, which makes for a bigger, more comfortable motorcycle without the expense and trouble of stretching the frame. A longer swingarm will, however, create the need for a longer chain or belt (some longer belts are available, but a longer swingarm may necessitate a switch to chain drive).

Before cutting into the neck area to change the rake, remember that the factory box-section, often built up of more than one layer, is

This is the "before" picture of a stock late-model Sporty frame seen at M-C Specialties. Because of the frame design, it's hard to simply "rake" this frame.

So instead, the M-C crew cut away much of the down tubes and webbed area just behind the neck (though they saved the neck itself), and created a front section that provides a clean look and additional rake.

extremely strong. So at the risk of my being redundant, make sure the new frame section is as strong as the factory stuff you're replacing.

Painting and Molding the Frame

If you paint the frame you make more work for yourself, but you also open the door to a whole host of new creative possibilities. The color of the frame can now match or complement the overall paint job. The frame becomes more a part of the total design instead of something to be worked around. For those who "step up" and make the decision to paint the frame, there comes a series of related decisions that follow.

The first decision involves whether or not to mold or disguise all those ugly factory welds. The second decision involves the type of paint to be used on the frame. As always, the two decisions are interrelated.

Molding the frame gives the bike that professional look, the look that says you went the extra mile and spared no expense. But even after the bike is stripped to the bare frame the molding is a lot of work, especially for the virgins in the group who have never molded a frame before. (See the sidebar for more on molding.)

Because the frame is subject to rock chips and abuse, the paint you use needs to be as durable as possible. The two logical paint choices are urethane and powder paint. Urethane paints are the most durable of the liquid paint systems. The isocyanate catalyst used with these paints means the molecules are cross-linked and form a very tough and durable film. As tough as urethanes are, they don't stand up to road use like powder-painted components.

Powder paint is essentially pulverized plastic that is "sprayed" onto your frame with help from an electrostatic charge. Once the paint is applied, the parts are loaded into an oversize pizza oven where the bake cycle causes the powder material to bond with the metal underneath.

The electrostatic charge and the heat mean that the frame must be made entirely of metal in order to be correctly powder coated. Any "molding" you do to a frame prior to powder coating must be done in metal and then metal finished. Instead of working with plastic filler, you now need to work with a metal filler like Aluma-lead or do your molding with phosphor bronze welding rod. (See the sidebar in Chapter 8 for more on powder coating.)

The powder paints come in a full rainbow of colors, and even clear coats. Matching the color used on the sheet metal can be hard, however, so it's easier to have the frame done first and then match that color with the liquid paint system used on the tank(s) and fenders.

Rounding It Up

Before stripping the bike to the bare frame, take a long look at the money and time you have dedicated to this project. Painting and possibly molding the frame add both to the professional look of the finished bike and to the total cost of the project.

If you decide to pull it all the way down and paint and modify the frame, make sure you allow enough time and choose the right shop for any actual frame work. Recently I had a fella tell me about the first "chopper" he built some years back, and how the frame broke at the neck while he was accelerating down the ramp onto the freeway. He lived to tell the tale but you can bet he's learned to be careful about who does the modifications on his frames.

In the end, frame work is just like all the other parts of this bike building business: you have to be sure to budget enough time and dollars, and pick the subcontractors with care.

CHAPTER 4 SUSPENSION AND BRAKES

Contents

Front Forks 26

Changing Forks 26

Springs and Shocks 27

Lowering the Bike:
How Short Is Too Short? . .29

Fat Is Where It's At 30

Brakes 31

Big-Wheel Conversion 32

The goal of any suspension system is to isolate the structure from shocks and vibrations generated as the wheels move over the road surface. The suspension system must also provide stability and overall control of the vehicle, and ensure that the tires stay in contact with the road. It's not as simple as it might seem, especially when you consider that a motorcycle is essentially "hinged" in the middle.

Though all Harley-Davidsons use a front fork of the standard "right-side up" configuration, the rear suspensions come in two very different styles.

Front Forks

Your choice of a fork assembly is dictated by what you see in the magazines and what came with the bike. But first a few terms: "wide glide" and "narrow glide" simply refer to the distance between the two fork tubes. The wide glide, for example, measures nearly ten inches center-to-center (exact dimensions vary between Dyna and Softail models). Softails come with a wide-glide fork while most (though not all) Dyna, FXR, and Sportster models run narrow-glide forks. A vast array of fork tubes and triple trees have been used at one time or another by the factory. But we will limit the discussion to late model offerings, in which case the number of possible units is more reasonable.

There are two fork-tube diameters offered by Harley-Davidson in current use: 39 mm and 41 mm

(1987-and-earlier FXRs and Sportsters used a 35-mm fork tube). The 39-mm tubes are normally run in the narrow-glide configuration and are used on Sportsters and some Dyna models. This size was also used on FXRs from 1988 to the end of production. This fork assembly comes from the factory in three lengths, with provisions for single or dual disc brakes.

The 41-mm forks come in three basic versions: FLT, Softail Custom, and Heritage (also Fat Boy). The FLT (or "dresser") tubes are the shortest, with Heritage next in length and Softail Custom being the longest of all. Of course longer and (sometimes) shorter tubes are available in most styles from the various aftermarket companies. Or you can call Forking by Frank for a custom tube of any length. If you want dual discs on a 41-mm fork, you have to either run FL-style lower fork legs with factory attaching points for the calipers or use aftermarket calipers with their own mounting system.

A few final notes on forks. More exotic upside-down forks are available from White Brothers, and lightweight Ceriani forks are available from Storz. Before buying a swap-meet fork assembly, remember that the lower triple tree has a number stamped in it that matches the bike it was originally bolted to.

Changing Forks

The neck and fork-stem bearings are the same on all late model

Dressers use 41-mm tubes in a Wide Glide configuration. Typical dresser lower legs have caliper mounting lugs on both sides. The fork tubes used for dressers are the shortest of all the factory 41-mm fork configurations.

Big Twins and Sportsters. In theory, any triple tree should work on any frame. There are, however, a few additional considerations.

The 1988 and later FXR chassis are set up to run 39-mm narrow-glide forks. When you try to put a set of factory wide-glide triple trees and 41mm fork tubes on one of these frames, part of the lower triple tree contacts the down tubes just below the neck. The way out of this dilemma is found by trimming away material (the lock tab and surrounding metal) from the stock wide-glide triple tree so it can be substituted for the narrow-glide triple tree. There is no problem when going the other way, or bolting a narrow-glide onto a frame that normally runs a wide-glide fork assembly.

If you already have 39-mm fork legs but want a wide-glide front end, you can buy aftermarket triple trees like those from Ness. These billet aluminum trees allow you to run 39-mm fork legs in a wide-glide configuration. There are even some aftermarket triple trees that effectively change the rake so you don't have to cut and weld the neck.

Before changing to a new fork assembly, consider that all the components that make up the front end of the bike must be designed (or modified) to work with all the other parts. A wide-glide fork will require the proper wheel hub, or at least the right spacers, and the right brackets or spacers to mount the front fender. When changing triple trees, make sure the lower tree has a provision for a fork stop, either something that will match the factory tab on the neck or another means of limiting fork travel.

Springs and Shocks

Coil springs of the type used on both ends of most Harley-Davidsons are rated according to how much weight it takes to compress the

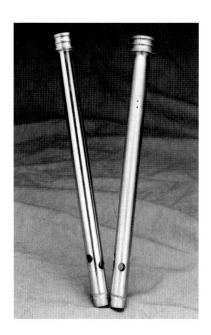

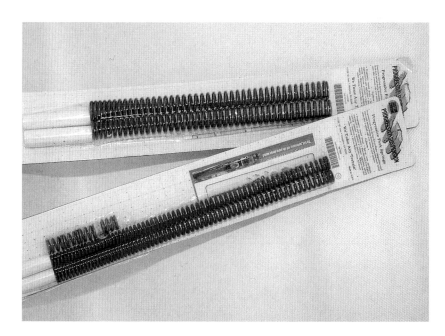

Stock 39-mm fork assemblies offer shock damping on compression only, not on rebound. These damper tubes from Progressive Suspension offer damping on rebound and thus improve the handling and feel of your motorcycle. *Custom Chrome*

You can lower the front end and firm up the ride with a Progressive spring kit, available to fit most factory fork assemblies.

spring a given amount. Without some kind of damping, any spring will oscillate up and down after hitting a bump until all the energy absorbed by the bump is dissipated. Thus each spring needs a damper, or shock absorber, to ensure that the bike doesn't "pogo" down the road.

In the world of motorcycles the spring and shock absorber are usually combined into one unit. The front fork tubes contain oil and a damper rod and thus function as a shock absorber. At the rear, most springs are actually wound around the shock absorber. Shock absorbers used on motorcycles are really nothing more than a piston, usually with small holes or spring-loaded one-way valves, moving through a volume of oil of a specific viscosity.

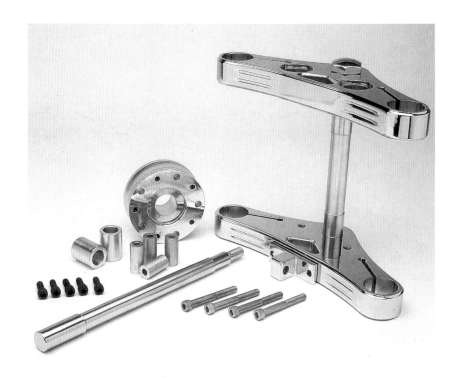

If your bike has a narrow-glide fork with 39-mm fork tubes and you want the look of a wide-glide, use a billet triple tree set like this one to create a 39-mm wide-glide fork assembly. *Arlen Ness Inc.*

When this shock absorber works too hard the piston moves rapidly though the oil, first in one direction and then the other. This rapid piston movement causes the oil to overheat and also creates cavitation at the piston. The net effect is aerated oil, and a "faded" shock absorber that does little to dampen spring movement. To prevent overheating, some shocks use aluminum bodies because aluminum more easily dissipates heat to the surrounding air. Another approach, known as "gas charging," uses an inert gas to pressurize the oil and thus prevent aeration.

When considering new or modified suspension components for your Harley-Davidson, remember that while cheap or worn-out components on a car might only cause it to wallow, on a motorcycle a wallow can lead to a wobble—the dreaded speed wobble.

Lowering the Bike: How Short Is Too Short?

We all want our bikes "slammed." Before having four inches cut off the tubes (more later), think about your overall plan for the bike, the effect of any increase to the rake, any planned change in wheel diameter, and the way in which you ride. There is no simple slide-rule or computer program for determining the right fork or shock length.

People who ride hard like to have as much as seven inches of clearance between the bottom of the frame tubes and the ground, even though most factory Softails don't have that much clearance. The low-and-slow crowd often get by with as little as four inches of clearance between the tubes and the tar.

If what you're doing is lowering an otherwise stock Harley-Davidson, it's pretty easy to predict the effect of a given lowering kit. If you elect instead to change the rake and install a new fork

Progressive offers their 412-series shocks (on the left) in either black or chrome. A variety of springs are available to help tailor the shock to the individual rider. Koni offers their premium shocks (right) with adjustments for both pre-load and valving during rebound and compression. Both shocks are available in a variety of lengths.

You can now convert your Softail to adjustable torsion-bar suspension. The kit includes a new, single shock absorber, the torsion bar, and all necessary mounting hardware. *Drag Specialties*

assembly, you need to spend time mocking the bike up on the hoist and asking questions when you buy the components.

Lowering the front of the bike can be done by cutting the tubes, installing shorter tubes, or installing a spring kit designed to lower the front of the bike. Custom Chrome, Drag Specialties, Chrome Specialties, and most of the others offer new fork tubes, both shorter and longer than stock. Both Progressive Suspension and White Brothers offer spring kits that will drop the front of most late model Harleys up to two inches. When reassembled, the fork will be shorter than stock and have reduced suspension travel as well. White Brothers claims that this is a safer way of lowering the front of your Harley because the kit lowers the bike *and* reduces suspension travel—so the bike "bottoms" where it did before (with the frame the same distance from the ground) and is less likely to drag the chassis across those bad bumps. Even Harley-Davidson offers two different kits to lower your Sportster or Dyna with 39-mm forks.

Most late-model fork-tube and triple-tree combinations also allow you to slide the tube up in the triple trees and thus lower the front of the chassis. Done in moderation or on bikes with a fairing to hide the tube sticking up above the top triple tree, this offers one more option for lowering the bike.

At the back of a twin-shock Harley-Davidson the lowering process is fairly simple and is usually accomplished by installing shorter shock absorbers. Your local Harley dealer or independent shop can sell you rear shocks for non-Softail Harleys that are one, two, or three inches shorter than stock.

If you buy shorter shocks, buy the best-quality shocks you can afford. Companies like White Brothers, Progressive Suspension, and

To lower the rear of your dresser without resorting to shorter shocks or inverted swingarms, try these White Brothers lowering kits, which relocate the lower shock mounts. *Drag Specialties*

Works Performance offer gas-charged shocks that offer a better ride and increased resistance to fade—in a variety of lengths and styles.

The Harley Softail bikes feature rear suspension that is very different than the more conventional suspension offered on the other models. Unlike FXRs and Dynas, the Softail bikes hide the two shock/spring units under the gearbox. While the other shock/springs push against the swingarm, those hidden under the Softail's gearbox pull on the triangulated swingarm.

This novel suspension design requires a different approach when it comes to lowering the bike. The Softail bikes also start life physically lower than the other Harley models (like the FXR or Dyna series, for example) and start to drag relatively easily if the bike is lowered too far.

A variety of kits from all the major suspension manufacturers allow the Softail owner to drop the back of the bike one inch or more. Some kits allow the owner to adjust the suspension to suit the situation, from a half-inch higher to two inches lower.

Remember that even before you lower the back of that Softail, the suspension only offers about three inches of travel. Many riders find that quality aftermarket shocks make better use of the Softail's limited travel, providing a better overall ride and less bottoming.

Relatively new on the market is a torsion-bar suspension for Softails. Available in three strengths, the system is adjustable and uses a single shock absorber to dampen the action of the torsion bar.

As always, any suspension work you do must include a check to ensure that with the new components in place the tire can't possibly touch the fender, the fender mounting bolts, or any other hardware inside or under the fender.

Fat Is Where It's At

Among all the fads that come and go, nothing is more popular than the current passion for fat rear tires. In fact, what seemed like a really wide rear tire two or three years ago looks like a skinny antique tire today.

The only problem with this trend to wider and wider rear tires is the difficulty in mounting one in a stock frame and swingarm. Most Softails, for example, come from the factory with a 130/90x16-inch rear tire. Clever owners and customizers have managed to replace those skinny tires with 140-series rubber without too much trouble. Any tire much wider than a 140, however, usually runs into the drive belt. Sure, you can trade in the belt for a chain, but most riders want a wide rear tire *and* the convenience of belt drive.

Basically, there are two ways to go when it comes to modifying the bike to accept a tire more than one or two sizes larger than stock. Your first option is to keep the rear wheel pulley lined up with the transmission pulley and move the wheel to the right slightly. Moving the wheel to the right a small amount doesn't seem to cause any handling problems as long as the offset is small (like a quarter-inch), though the degree to which it affects the handling depends on whom you talk to. This type of offset does affect procedures used for checking alignment of the wheels.

Donnie Smith has used this trick to install 150- and 160-series tires in the back of FXR chassis for some time. He simply machines a small amount (0.200 in for FXR and 0.250 in for Softails) off the inside of the caliper mount, which moves the wheel to the right, and then adds a spacer of the same dimension to the other side between the pulley and the wheel hub.

Option number two is to leave the rear wheel in its stock location relative to the engine and front wheel, and move the wheel pulley to the left to clear the belt. Now you have to move the transmission pulley over to the left as well, so it

will line up with the wheel pulley. Moving the transmission pulley to the left means moving the transmission, or the engine and transmission, to the left as well.

The exact parts and procedures you use here depend on the frame type. Because Softails mount the engine and transmission to the frame as separate units, it's possible to move only the transmission to the left with a special kit.

"Wide Tire" Softail kits from Arlen Ness and others provide an offset transmission mounting plate and a group of spacers that move the whole transmission and inner primary over to the left to make room between the belt and the wider tire. Rubber-mount bikes like Dynas and FXRs have their engine and transmissions bolted together as a unit and require a very different kit, one that moves the entire engine-transmission package to the left to create enough belt clearance.

Chrome Specialties has taken the idea of moving the Softail primary to the left one step further with its new X-Drive swingarm, designed by Smith. Now the tire you really want—as wide as 7-5/8 inches across—can be installed in a stock Harley-Davidson Softail frame. Like the other kits, this one moves the primary and the belt to the left. But by including a new swingarm in the kit, Chrome Specialties has created more room for the belt to move to the left—and thus more room for the tire that looks like it came off a Pro Street bike instead of a Schwinn.

If all this installation of spacers and swingarms sounds like too much work, the other option is to trade in the belt for a chain. Sprockets, including offset sprockets, and kits intended for this application can be found in nearly any aftermarket catalog.

Don't forget that the stock fenders are designed for stock-sized tires. Even one size bigger

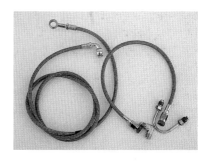

On the left is a complete pre-made line from Russell, available to fit a number of stock or near-stock applications. On the right is a hose from Goodridge, which requires that you start with the right length and then use the correct adapter on each end. Both these hoses are the Plus-3 size. Note: Not all fittings/threads are the same so always try to buy all the components from one manufacturer.

might well rub on the inside of the fender. Your new fat tire will probably need a fat fender and new struts as well. And if you move the tire over to the right it will no longer be centered under the fender. Be sure the tire can't rub on the inside of the fender and remember that tires grow and change in size as the speed of the bike increases.

For more on fat tire installation, see the accompanying sidebar.

Brakes

Brakes are essentially heat machines—converting the moving or kinetic energy of your motorcycle to heat. When planning how substantial the brakes are that you buy. It might be instructive to remember that when you double the speed of a vehicle you create four times the kinetic energy. When buying brakes for a high performance motorcycle, more is better. More rotor surface area, more pistons per caliper (usually with larger pads as well) and, in some cases, more calipers. The

BIG-WHEEL CONVERSION

This installation sequence shows an Arlen Ness Big Wheel conversion kit installed in a 1988 Softail owned by Gary Schallock, loyal employee of Kokesh MC in Spring Lake Park, Minnesota. Schallock decided to mount the kit as part of an overall upgrade plan for the old Softail—so don't think you have to pull your bike down as far as he did just to have a wide rear tire.

1 This shot shows the typical Softail shock absorber layout. Installation of the kit requires disassembly of the primary drive and removal of the transmission. The engine on this 1988 FXSTC was apart for other hop-up work. Once the transmission is removed, the transmission mount on the far right (the one perched above the right shock) must have its hole enlarged. Sometimes, the stud that passes through this hole must be trimmed so it will not hit the shock.

2 Looking at the bottom of the transmission, the new offset transmission plate has been bolted on in place of the original.

3 The spacer plate mounts between the engine case and the inner primary, with an O-ring used on either side.

4 To ensure that the engine and transmission are aligned properly relative to each other, it's best to leave the transmission-to-frame mounting bolts snug, then install and tighten the inner primary to the engine and transmission bolts, and finally tighten the transmission-to-frame bolts. As a good double check, once the transmission mounting bolts are tight you should be able to slide the inner primary off and on without any force.

5 Gary is mounting a 170/60x18 Avon tire to a rim that's 4-1/4 inches wide. Because a 170 is on the edge of what will fit even with the offset kit, the rim was laced with just a little offset to the right so the tire is sure to clear the belt.

6 A spacer must also be used between the compensator sprocket and the engine so the primary chain is moved over as much as everything else.

7 The kit includes a spacer that mounts between the inside of the drive sprocket and the outside of the rear hub. The basic idea is to leave the centerline of the tire in its stock location and move the belt pulley to the left.

downside to more brakes is the expense, complexity, and additional unsprung weight.

Bill Gardner from GMA Brakes in Omaha, Nebraska, offers an interesting insight into this whole business of improving the brakes. "When people upgrade their brakes they do it to gain stopping ability, but they also gain something more subtle. They gain a better feel of what's going on; they are better able to modulate the brake. With stock brakes it's more of an on or off situation."

The brake discussion here is limited to disc brakes, because unless you are restoring an old Panhead or early Shovelhead, the brakes, especially the front brake(s), should be disc and not drum. If you're going to make it go faster you've got to make it stop better as well. The front wheel has at least 70 percent of the stopping power, so spend your money improving the brakes on the front wheel first.

This is the prototype swingarm built by Donnie Smith and marketed under the X-Drive trade name by Chrome Specialties. By moving the left side vertical support to the inside, this swingarm makes room for a very wide tire while leaving clearance for the stock belt drive.

Here you see the X-Drive swingarm on the nearly finished prototype bike. Note how the belt runs between the frame and the swingarm. Essentially this allows the belt to run much farther to the left than would be possible with a stock frame and swingarm combination.

There's a current retro-chopper bike-building trend going on. Riders are building bikes that look just like they did 25 years ago, complete with the long front ends and no front brakes. Just because the builders of the original choppers often went without front brakes doesn't mean you should. Whatever you build, make it functional and safe to ride—put some good brakes on the front end.

Deciding exactly what type of brakes to install opens a vast number of options. The catalogs from Drag Specialties, Custom Chrome, Chrome Specialties, Arlen Ness, and many more are crammed full of master cylinders, calipers, and rotors. Well-known companies like Performance Machine, JayBrake, and GMA build two-, four-, and six-piston calipers, rotors in a variety of styles and materials, and master cylinders in a host of configurations.

The X-Drive swingarm as seen in Donnie Smith's shop with a 200-series 16-inch tire from Avon. This kit, which includes the swingarm and all necessary hardware (but not the wider rear fender you will require), allows you to run a tire measuring up to 7-5/8 inches across. Note that the width of a given tire is determined in-part by how wide a rim it is mounted on.

Making the best choice from among this rather bewildering array of options will depend on your riding style, budget, and the design for your motorcycle.

Perry Sands from Performance Machine says they often get calls from riders who want to know if they should buy a four- or six-piston caliper and, in some cases, which four-piston caliper is best for their application.

"When people call us with questions about brakes, I start by asking them what type of riding they do," Sands says. "Does he or she pack double or is it a single-seat custom? When you consider brakes, the weight or mass is an important issue. A Softail with a skinny 21-inch tire may need less front brake than a Road King that gets used on mountain roads—it's hard to get too much brake on that bigger, heavier bike.

"The four-piston caliper is our standard. What makes the difference between ours and the single-piston caliper that comes with the bikes is that by adding pistons we're able to use a bigger, longer pad and relocate it to the outer area on the rotor. It does the most good there because it has more leverage. In that sense, four pistons are good, six are better."

In terms of upgrading the brakes and getting the most for your money, Sands recommends the following progression: Start by replacing the stock caliper with one of their four-piston calipers. The next step for most people is to move up to a larger diameter rotor. If the bike in question has a single front brake you can probably add two brakes with 11.5 inch rotors and four piston calipers, complete with the new lower fork leg, for not much more than you can buy a real trick single rotor set up with large diameter rotor and six-piston caliper.

Sands goes on to explain that the trick, single-rotor setup has a handling advantage due to having only 50 percent of the unsprung weight, and it's a direct bolt-on upgrade.

Relatively new to the PM line is a differential bore, four-piston caliper designed to be used with 11.5 inch rotors. These new calipers are designed to be used by either the high-performance street guy who likes to ride really fast or the touring person. Differential bore simply means the caliper uses a smaller-diameter leading piston, which evens out the pad temperature.

"Normally there's a lot more heat at the front edge of pad," explains Sands. "It might be 200 to 300 degrees hotter there. These calipers are more powerful and they're good for extreme heat situations. My Road King is equipped with the new calipers and they work really nice. My wife and I rode through Yellowstone on the way to Sturgis. On the east side of the park we had 20 miles of aggressive downhill riding with plenty of corners and lots of brake use. With a maximum effort of two fingers on the brake lever we had consistent feel and no brake fade."

At this point we should add that floating, stainless-steel rotors are available from the factory. Your local dealer can also assist if you want to add a second brake to the front of a Harley that came equipped with only one rotor and caliper. "We have a kit for the Sportsters, Dynas, and FXRs equipped with the 39-mm narrow-glide fork," explains George Edwards of St. Paul Harley-Davidson. "The kit includes everything you need: the second caliper, rotor, lower fork leg, the hose, and even the new master cylinder with the correct bore size.

"Adding a second brake to the wide-glide bikes with 41-mm forks is harder to do," adds Edwards. "You would have to buy complete fork-tube assemblies from the

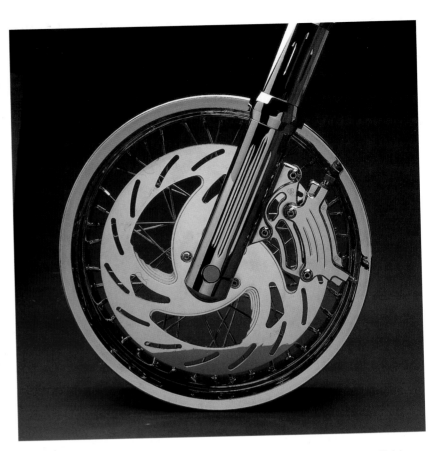

Built by Performance Machine, these Arlen Ness calipers are available either polished or chrome-plated. Slotted, swept rotors are a full 13 inches in diameter. Note the trick billet lower leg. *Arlen Ness Inc.*

dresser line; those lower legs have the lugs to mount dual calipers. Then you've still got to buy everything else.

"The nice thing about running Harley-Davidson parts instead of aftermarket parts, though, is their availability. If you need pads when you're out on the road, it's a lot easier to find a dealer with the factory pad than a new set of pads for some aftermarket caliper. And of course all the factory stuff is DOT certified."

Most factory rotors are made from stainless steel. The aftermarket, however, offers rotors made from stainless, cast iron, and even ductile iron. Stainless steel might seem to be the ideal material for brake rotors until you consider the fact that cast or ductile iron makes

a much better friction material. Once again the rotor that's right for your custom Softail might not be the right one for a hard riding Sportster rider.

Bill Gardner, owner of GMA Brakes, explains that the stainless rotors all come from one company in Japan. "Basically these are made from cold-rolled steel with some chrome added to it. It's a very hard material but it has a couple of problems. First, the nature of the material is such that it's prone to certain harmonics or vibrations, which we hear as a squeal. Second, the hardness doesn't give the pads anything very good to grab onto, the coefficient of friction is about 20 or 30 percent lower than cast iron."

Cast iron and ductile iron both offer the brake pad a softer, rougher

Carved from 6061 T6 billet aluminum, these four-piston calipers combine form and function. Available polished or chrome-plated, with or without the logo, to fit nearly any Harley-Davidson application. *Custom Chrome*

surface to grab onto. Both materials are very durable. Gardner likes the ductile iron because of its extreme toughness and the material's ability to radiate the heat of multiple hard stops to the surrounding air. The proverbial trade-off is the tendency of either cast or ductile iron to rust if the bike sits too much or lives in damp environments like the coast of Florida. And while a stainless rotor might last for 100,000 miles, an iron rotor will only survive for 60,000 or 70,000 miles.

No matter which rotor material you choose, there needs to be a good match between pad and rotor material. Pad materials used on the street break down into two groups. First there are the organic materials, which means a non-metallic pad (Kevlar pads are part of this first group). The other

commonly used material is metallic or sintered-iron pads.

"Because the ductile iron is a softer material, we recommend nonmetallic brake pads," explains Gardner. "This is actually a racing pad, an 'RQ' Compound, a Kevlar-type material. It's a relatively soft material and it gives improved feel and stops well, except that it isn't real good in wet weather. We also offer a sintered-iron, high-friction pad. It works good in wet weather but it's harder on rotors. Stainless rotors are so tough you can run any pad, including the metallic materials. In fact you can improve the braking of a bike with stainless rotors by switching from an organic to a metallic pad."

Though a polished stainless rotor might look great on your sexy new ride, don't take the concept of

polishing one step further and chrome plate the rotors. Anyone who does soon discovers that the ultra smooth surface gives the brake pad nothing to grip and stopping power suffers in the extreme. And if that weren't enough, polishing and plating can warp the rotor.

If you intend to replace both calipers and master cylinders, you need to match the new caliper(s) to the master cylinder bore size. Essentially, a smaller diameter master cylinder piston creates more hydraulic pressure but displaces less fluid than a larger diameter piston (all other things being equal). Thus if the hydraulic ratios aren't correctly matched between the master cylinder and calipers, you could end up with high-effort brakes, or a master cylinder with too small a piston that doesn't displace enough fluid to fully apply the brakes.

Gardner offers the following rule of thumb: With a single new caliper, rear or front, use a master cylinder with a 5/8-inch bore. If you have dual calipers on the front, whether they're four- or six-piston calipers, use a master cylinder with a 3/4-inch piston bore. If in doubt, ask the salesperson or manufacturer of your new brake components for a recommendation."

Connecting the master cylinder(s) to the calipers are the flexible brake lines. As the bike ages these lines tend to crack and may need to be replaced. Because the hydraulic pressure in the brake system approaches 1,000 psi, only hoses approved for use in hydraulic brake systems may be used. When owners upgrade the brakes they often replace the factory hoses with braided stainless lines from companies like Russell. The braided lines use Teflon inner liners to actually carry the fluid. Unlike the factory hoses, which may swell just slightly with brake application, the Teflon liners do not expand even a little under hard

CHAPTER 5

WHEELS AND TIRES

Contents

What's a Billet? 40

Rim Sizes 43

Different Spokes for
Different Folks 44

Hooking Up to
the Asphalt 47

Making the
Final Decision 48

Wheels and tires are a major part of your newly constructed motorcycle. The wheels have a major impact on a bike's handling and looks, and they certainly can have a major impact on your checking account as well. Possible choices include billet, cast, and spoked wheels. While the new billet beauties offer a certain flash and style, spoked wheels have a traditional appeal that's hard to deny.

Like everything else, choosing wheels is a matter of design and budget. If billet wheels are ultra modern, a 40-spoke wheel with an Akront rim is a thing of classic beauty.

What's a Billet?

They all go by the name "billet," but that doesn't mean they're all the same in terms of strength, weight, and price. In reality what we call billet wheels come in at least three distinctly different flavors—but first a little history.

Motorcycle trends often follow automotive trends (at least lately) and it's Boyd Coddington, the original Big Wheel, who gets the credit for putting the first pair of billet wheels on a street rod in about 1981. Actually, it was Boyd's friend Lil' John Buttera who first combined an existing rim with a center section cut and shaped from a piece of solid (or billet) aluminum.

Buttera cut those first center sections from the same material that most billet wheel manufacturers use today, 6061 T6 aluminum. The number "6061" identifies this particular alloy, which in reality is very durable, forged aluminum that can still be machined and polished with relative ease. The designation "T6" is the heat-treating specification. The first wheels were cut on a Bridgeport mill, though Boyd soon discovered that you could turn out more wheels with less labor on a CNC machine.

Despite all the labor saved by cutting the wheels on automated equipment, billet wheels are still expensive. The reason is the cost of the high-grade aluminum, combined with the fact that even with automated equipment there is still plenty of machine time invested in each wheel. In addition to the cutting and polishing, each center section must be welded or bolted to a rim and then trued, or at least checked to ensure the wheel is straight and round.

If it's the labor and material costs that make a billet wheel expensive, why not reduce both by casting the wheels? Thus was born the less expensive "billet" wheel cast from 356 aluminum. These wheels have the look everyone wants without the high cost of 6061 aluminum, the wasted material, and the machine time on the CNC mills.

Billet motorcycle wheels are currently rolling down some of the same paths as the automotive wheels, propelled in fact by some of the same players, with just a few unique two-wheeled twists to keep everything interesting. As in the automotive market, the billet wheels seen in all the motorcycle

The style of your bike helps to determine which wheel and tire combination look best. This modern chopper uses the very traditional skinny 21-inch front tire and fat, 150-series 16-inch Dunlop in the rear.

The center sections of billet wheels can be either bolted or welded to the rim (some are one-piece) By bolting the center section to the rim there is no heat and no potential for warpage. *Mid-USA*

catalogs come in both true billet designs and in cast designs that look like billet and cost considerably less.

When trying to decide between a billet and a cast wheel, remember that it's hard to beat the strength-to-weight ratio of 6061 aluminum. This means that in most cases a true billet wheel is lighter and stronger than a very similar-appearing cast wheel. And cast wheels may not be able to match the polished finish seen on a billet wheel. Because of the strength of 6061, billet wheels offer designs and details that simply can't be matched with a cast design.

A potential problem with billet wheels is the way in which the rim (usually a separate part) is attached to the center section. Welding, and then polishing the weld, leaves a clean no-see-um seam, but the welding has the potential to distort the wheel. Cast one-piece wheels avoid this potential problem but don't have the strength of forged aluminum. Perhaps the best of both worlds is offered by new one-piece billet wheels in which the rim and wheel are cut from a single piece of billet aluminum. These offer the seamless look of a welded aluminum wheel without the welding.

In the motorcycle market there is a third type of aluminum wheel, and this wheel type is known as spun aluminum. Spun aluminum wheels are made by combining two halves, made from relatively thin aluminum sheet, with a hub cut from solid aluminum stock. Each half of the wheel is "spun" or rolled into a specific shape—essentially a shallow dome with a flair at the outer edge. The flange at the outer edge forms half the rim. Next, the two halves are clamped and welded together. Now all the wheel needs is a hub of the correct dimension added at the center, and the machining of any designs or slots into the surface. Spun aluminum wheels are very light and very strong, though not all the major players offer them.

There are a few more things to consider when you buy those new billet wheels. First, get what you pay for. If you're paying billet prices, be sure the wheels are in fact billet aluminum. Second, not all bolt-in wheels do. Ask around at some local shops to learn which wheels fit the first time and which don't. Third, give some thought as to which finish you want on those wheels. A polished aluminum wheel comes with a brilliant finish, but it won't always look that good unless you're handy with the Simichrome or other polish. More and more wheel manufacturers are offering their designs in chrome-plated versions. The other option is to have the wheel clear-coated so you can have the look of polished aluminum without the maintenance. Some

By carving both the center and the rim from a single billet of aluminum, there is no need to bolt the rim to the center section, or create runout by welding the two together. All you need now is a matching billet hub. *Arlen Ness Inc.*

Less expensive than billet, these one-piece cast designs from Drag Specialties come in a variety of 16-inch widths and even a few 17-inch sizes. *Drag Specialties*

powder coating operations offer powder-coat clear, which should provide a really durable finish that shines but won't oxidize (see the sidebar in Chapter 8 for more on powder coating).

When it comes to looking for a new set of wheels, consider all the sources, including your local Harley-Davidson dealer. Through the accessories catalog, Harley offers a variety of cast wheels in standard finish or with a chrome finish. Some innovative builders take a solid factory wheel, from a Fat Boy, for example, to the mill and create a really unique design without the cost of buying billet.

Rim Sizes

Up until recently the common wheel sizes used on Harley-Davidson motorcycles were 21, 19, and 16 inches for the front, and 16 inches for the rear. With the phenomenal growth in the custom-

This is the rear tire and wheel combination used in the Big Wheel sidebar in Chapter 4. The tire is a 170/60x18 from Avon. The Akront rim is 4-1/4 inches wide, the hub is stock Harley-Davidson, and the spokes are from Buchanan. A good shop can lace the wheel with an offset, which was used in this case to help ensure that the tire would clear the belt.

Chrome-plated Akront rims are available in assembled form, complete with chrome-plated spokes and hub. Various widths are available in 16-, 18-, 19-, and 21-inch diameters. *Custom Chrome*

wheel market, the "standard" diameters have grown to include 17 and 18 inches. In particular, while stock late model bikes commonly run a 130/90x16-inch rear tire, the current trend is to larger rubber for that fat look. Many riders are replacing the 130-series, 16-inch rear tires with 140-, 150-, and even 200-series rubber. Though the really wide 170, 180, and 200 sizes were originally seen only in 17- and 18-inch sizes, Avon now has a 200/60x16-inch rear tire, so you can have that wide rubber and keep the traditional 16-inch rear rim. (For more on fat-tire installations see the sidebar in this chapter.)

How fat that rear rubber should be is another decision that must be made early in the planning stage. Running anything wider than about a 140- or 150-series tire in back usually requires offset engine kits and/or modified swingarms.

DIFFERENT SPOKES FOR DIFFERENT FOLKS

THE OLD-FASHIONED SPOKED WHEEL IS NEVER OUT OF STYLE

The earliest motorcycles used spoked wheels, though instead of a 40-spoke aluminum rim with stainless steel spokes, these early bone-shakers relied on 10 or 12 spokes of oak supporting a solid wheel of wood or steel. By the turn of the century most motorcycles had settled into the modern pattern of using steel spokes to support a steel rim equipped with a pneumatic tire.

Almost 100 years later, the spoked wheel is alive and well, despite the abundance of ultra-modern billet designs currently on the market. In fact, there are probably more spoked wheel designs and sizes available today than at any other time.

Spoked wheels come in 40, 80, and 120 spoke designs (and some limited production wheels with more than 120 spokes), with rims of aluminum or steel. Rim diameters include 16, 17, 18, 19 and 21 inches, with widths that range from just over 2 inches to 6 inches across. Spokes come in steel or stainless, round, square, and twisted. If you don't find what you want, you just aren't looking hard enough. Though you might have decided on spoked wheels during the planning phase, deciding exactly which spoked wheel to run can be mighty confusing.

Even after you know the width of the rim and diameter of the wheel, it can still be tough to decide between all the offerings. To help relieve the confusion, it might be helpful to break a typical spoked wheel down into the three subassemblies and talk about each of those.

Hubs

At the center of the wheel is the hub, made from either steel or aluminum. Not all hubs are created equal, and not all hubs use the same spoke indexing pattern. Harley-Davidson has used at least three different indexing patterns over the years, including the new-for-1997 pattern. In addition, not all

Hubs are very specific in their application. This chrome-plated, single-flange hub is intended to fit Heritage Softails and Fat Boys. *Custom Chrome*

spokes will fit all hubs. The hub you use must match the bike's forks and brake configuration (that is, wide-glide or narrow-glide fork and single or double disc brakes). The hub manufacturer will suggest spokes; some are quite specific as to which spokes must be used with which hubs. Some of the sexiest wheels currently on the market are built around polished aluminum hubs.

Seen recently on some chopper-style bikes are spoked wheels with a straight-laced spoke pattern. Nearly all other indexing patterns use criss cross spoke patterns that give the wheel strength under acceleration or braking. Thus, the "new" straight-laced wheels are meant for front wheels with no brakes.

Spokes

Most of the spokes used today are 6/8 gauge, though heavier gauges are available for the burnout king or the person pulling a trailer. Materials include steel and stainless steel. George Edwards from St. Paul Harley-Davidson offered the opinion that the best spokes are either the plated factory spokes or the brand-name aftermarket offerings: "The worst seem to be the imported spokes; they seem to rust faster even if they're chrome plated and occasionally we see one break."

The name that comes up again and again when discussing spokes is Buchanan. These polished stainless spokes are made in the good

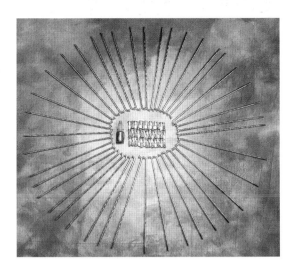

These American-made, stainless steel spokes are from Landmark, designed to fit 21-inch drop-center rims. *Drag Specialties*

old US of A and come in round, diamond, and twisted-rectangular designs. Each set of Buchanan spokes even comes with a small tube of anti-seize, and if the anti-seize is applied as recommended, there's no chance of corrosion where the spoke threads onto the nipple. Again, not all spokes fit all rims or hubs.

Rims

"When it comes to steel or aluminum rims," explains Gary Strom from Kokesh M-C, "I think the aluminum rims are a little stronger. It's hard to find good steel rims, though the factory Harley rims are pretty good." Perhaps the best known of the high-end aluminum rims come from Spain under the brand name Akront. Sun is another manufacturer of quality aluminum rims, though the manufacturer uses a smooth no-dimple design. Aluminum rims come in a vast array of sizes, all the way from 1.85x21 inches to 5.5x18 inches and 5x16 inches.

Chrome-plated steel rims come from a variety of manufacturers and are listed in every aftermarket catalog. Sizes of the steel rims tend to stay close to the most popular stock dimensions, though extra-wide 5x16-inch steel rims are available from a variety of sources.

To Lace or Not to Lace

Harley-Davidson riders tend to be "hands-on," and some want to lace their own wheels. Gary Strom from Kokesh, a man who has laced a lot of wheels, explains that "People ask how much it is to have the wheel laced, and then go home to try and do it themselves. A lot of those people are back the next day ready to pay us to lace the wheel. If they want to do the lacing at home that's O.K., but they should always take the truing to us or another good shop."

How Many Is Too Many?

American bikers think of themselves as trendsetters, but the zillion-spoked wheel deal started in Europe. Now we have 80- and 120-spoke wheels available here from a number of suppliers. If you think they look cool, then maybe you've got to have 'em. The downside is the extra weight of all those extra spokes and the fact that it always costs more to be cool.

Some of the new preassembled spoked wheels come in a tubeless design, made possible by using a heavy sealer in the center of the rim, which seals the nipples against the rim. This is a neat way to combine modern tubeless tires with traditional spoked wheels.

You don't have to start from scratch, of course. Unless you want something exotic or a rim with an unusual offset, there are some very high quality preassembled wheels on the market, both from Harley-Davidson and the aftermarket. Whether you want aluminum or steel rims, polished or chrome-plated, you can find it in a preassembled spoked wheel.

If you're assembling a wheel from scratch or looking to buy a preassembled wheel, consider these wise words of Mike McAllister from M-C Specialties: "Ask around at the various shops before you buy; find out who has the best rims and the best spokes. Some of the components are much better than others in terms of the quality and how well they fit. Remember that your whole life is riding on those wheels."

Fat bikes like this nice old Shovelhead look best with 16-inch tires on each end. Spoked wheels work well on this classic ride. Even though they might be the same size, front and rear tires have a very different profile and should never be swapped.

A number of quality aftermarket companies, including Arlen Ness, Sullivan Brothers, and Chrome Specialties (to name just a few) have brought out new swingarms for Softails designed to adapt a fairly wide tire, up to the 200x16, to a stock frame and retain the belt drive.

You have to understand that a 200x16 is a big round doughnut with a profile like the fat man with a beer belly, while a 180x18 is about the same outside diameter but has a slimmer, lower profile that will lend a different look to the bike. Remember that a given tire can be made wider or narrower according to how wide a rim it is mounted on.

Front tires tend to come in one of three diameters: 16, 19, or 21 inches. Dressers and "fat" bikes look good with the 16-inch tires while almost everything else seems to work best with the 19-inch tire and wheel combination. The 21-inch tires look good on chopper-style bikes, with or without a springer fork, and of course on the Softail Custom style bikes with wide-glide forks.

In the end, the bike's style and intended usage will dictate the size of the tires. But choosing the wheels and tires is another example of decisions that must be made in concert with all the other choices. A wide-glide fork will require the correct wheel hub and fender. A 21-inch wheel in place of a 19 will affect the ride height, which in turn affects your fork choice.

When you buy the wheels be sure to tell the dealer or counter person as much as you can about the bike. If it's a narrow-glide fork on an FXR with factory dual discs and you want to run a 90/90x19, tell them exactly that.

Hooking Up to the Asphalt

Which tire you put on that rim is going to depend on a number of factors, but for most of us it helps to install a tire that's about the same diameter as the stock tire. As Max Martin from Avon tire explains, "A low-profile 18-inch tire is about the same overall diameter as a 16-incher with a standard profile. So there's almost no change in gearing or in the clearance between the tire and the fender. The problem with 17-inch tires is that most are radials (more later) and even those that aren't are low-profile designs, so they end up being smaller in diameter than the tire that you took off the bike."

Though some sport and touring bikes carry radial tires, they aren't an option for your Harley-Davidson. Part of the reason is that there are no 19- or 21-inch radials, and you should not mix a radial on one end and a bias-ply tire on the other. Running a 140x16-inch radial intended for the rear on the front is also a very bad idea. "Don't ever run a rear radial on the front," says Martin. "You'll be all over the road because the rear radials are constructed in a very different way than the fronts."

You can run a bias-ply tire intended for the rear on the front of the bike, though it's not a good idea, as the steering slows down due to the very different shape of a rear tire as compared to the front.

All tires are rated according to speed and load capacity. Speed ratings are S, good for 112 miles per hour; H, good for 130 miles per

You might think your 150-series Metzeler (on the top) is a pretty meaty tire, until someone parks along side with a 200-series Avon (seen on the bottom). Most of the people running the 200 tire have mounted them in complete aftermarket frames or used swingarm kits to accommodate the ultra-fat rubber.

hour; and V, good for 150 miles per hour (a few inexpensive tires have no rating). Load ratings are B and C, with C being best suited to touring rigs with all their heavy paraphernalia.

Deciding which tire to put on the front and back of your ride is partly a matter of style. That is, do you like the "fat" look of a standard-profile tire or the slim "race" look of a low profile tire? Before deciding which is the perfect tire for your bike you need to know how wide it should be, as determined by the swingarm or fork, and the diameter of the rim. Now you can match that information with the size data published by the various tire manufacturers.

The data published by most manufacturers also lists the optimum rim width for each tire. By mounting a given tire on a wider rim, the tire does get wider, but

you can only go so far. For example, the 200/60x16-inch tire (currently Avon's widest tire) is 7.9 inches wide when mounted on the recommended 5.5-inch rim. The widest rim Avon recommends using with that tire is 6.25 inches wide, which will result in the same tire having a width of about 8.5 inches.

As stated earlier, each tire has a speed and load rating. To quote Martin again, "Most of the tires used by riders of custom bikes are rated at least S for speed and many are rated H or V. Most Harley riders don't run fast for long periods of time so for most riders the speed rating isn't critical. In terms of load ratings, the bikes are usually stripped so they're seldom overloaded. Where people should pay attention to the load rating is with a dresser. If you go from a stock 130/90x16-inch rear tire to a low

This very modern yellow Softail from Dave Perewitz uses equally modern Perewitz/Sullivan Brothers billet wheels in traditional 19- and 16-inch diameters. The rear rim is wide enough to accept the 200x16 Avon tire. Note the new Perewitz frame and the great Nancy Brooks graphic design.

profile 130/70x18, you've reduced the volume of air in the tire and thus the ability of that tire to carry a heavy load."

Making the Final Decision

As you plan out the new or modified bike, the choice of wheels and tires is one of the most important you will have to make. Not only do the wheels hold you up, they are a very large part of what anyone sees when they look at the bike.

So be a savvy buyer. First, make sure the new wheels and tires match your intended use. Second, buy something that fits your intended style, be it classic or ultra-modern. Third, ask around before buying to ensure you get the best quality and fit for your money.

CHAPTER 6   EVOLUTION HOP-UP

Contents

Carburetors 50

Which Carb Is for You? 53

What's Out There 54

A Final Note 55

Camshafts and Valve Gear .56

Putting It All Together 59

Which Camshaft Is
Right For You? 60

Ignition 60

Aftermarket Systems 60

A Computerized
Crystal Ball:
The Craig Walters
Accelerator Program 61

Engine Builders Speak Out . .62

Engine Case Studies 68

Building a hot V-twin for your Harley-Davidson is easier than ever, because each year there are more and more alternatives to choose from. The hard part is deciding exactly what to buy. You can either modify the engine that came with the bike, or start from scratch with a complete aftermarket engine. That aftermarket engine can be purchased as a complete assembly, as a kit, or you can put together your own kit with components from various manufacturers.

This engine chapter is meant to aid riders who want to extract extra power from the stock engine. The idea here is to help you get the maximum return, in terms of usable torque and horsepower, from your stock displacement Harley-Davidson engine. This chapter includes an overview of commonly used aftermarket components and interviews with two real-world V-twin mechanics. Near the end of this chapter are two engine-assembly case studies, one a Big Twin and the other a Sportster.

Chapter 7 deals with potentially larger and more exotic V-twins—engines displacing considerably more than 80 cubic inches. Included here is a short look at the old bore-versus-stroke controversy and a buyer's guide that covers the major parts and the best-known manufacturers.

Let's start our engine hop-up discussion by looking at some of the components you're most likely to replace in the quest for more horsepower.

Carburetors

A good carburetor is one that will supply a regulated quantity of air and fuel to the engine under all operating conditions. This means that no matter how hot or cold the engine is or how quickly you whack open the throttle, the engine will receive the correct amount of fuel for optimum operation.

At the heart of nearly any carburetor is a venturi, or a restriction of some kind in the carburetor throat. As Mr. Bernoulli discovered more than 200 years ago, when you force air through a restriction in a pipe the speed of the air increases as it moves through the restriction. As the velocity goes up the pressure goes down (think of the fast moving air as being "stretched" so it has less pressure). Now if we introduce gasoline at this low pressure point in the venturi, subject to atmospheric pressure at the other end, the gas will be "pushed" out into the airstream where it can atomize and mix with the air on its way to the cylinders.

The simple carburetor described above might work on a constant-speed engine, one that is always running and never changes speed. In the real world we need a means of controlling the flow of air through the carburetor and some additional fuel circuits. The extra circuits are handy for those

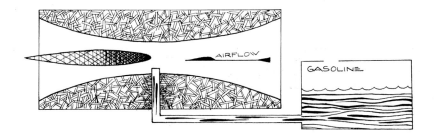

At the heart of every carburetor is a venturi, a restriction in a pipe. Air pressure within the venturi is reduced so the gas, which is under atmospheric pressure in the float bowl, flows to the venturi where it mixes and atomizes with air in the carburetor throat. *Ken Madden*

If you want to upgrade the exhaust, you can simply leave the stock header pipes in place and add new mufflers. Harley-Davidson offers both the turn-out design and the large touring muffler, which can be modified with different end caps.

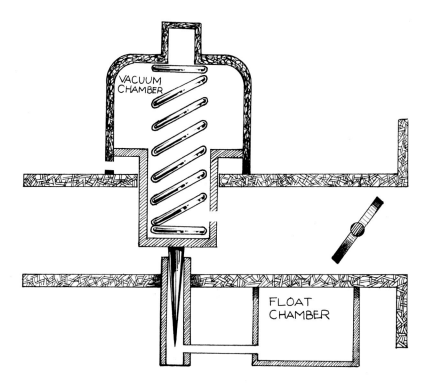

A Constant Velocity carburetor uses a vacuum-controlled slide and a standard throttle valve to control air moving through the carburetor throat. At idle a spring holds the slide closed, then, as the throttle is opened and engine rpm rises, increased engine vacuum pulls the slide up against spring pressure. The slide's upward movement pulls the tapered needle farther out of the main jet thus providing more fuel. Because the slide moves in relation to engine load and speed, the velocity of air in the carburetor throat stays constant, hence the name. In a pure "slide" carburetor there is no butterfly valve and the slide connects directly to the throttle cable. *Ken Madden*

occasions when there isn't enough air moving through the carb to create the vacuum needed to draw fuel from the venturi.

A good carburetor is designed to work in three "conditions," often described as idle, low speed, and high speed. Though many carburetors have these three basic circuits, and more, with air-bleeds and other provisions to ease the transition from one circuit to another, some are "seamless" examples that possess only one tapered needle that moves farther and farther out of the main jet in response to either throttle position or engine vacuum.

Even with a provision for controlling the airflow and various speeds, real-world carburetors have to deal with situations like cold starts and sudden acceleration. A cold engine needs an extra-rich mixture because gas doesn't like to atomize with cold air. Sudden acceleration, on the other hand, means the amount of air passing down the throat of the carburetor increases instantly, whereas the heavier fuel takes considerably longer to catch up.

So we add a choke or enrichment circuit for cold starts and an accelerator pump, though some carbs don't need one, to squirt a

Among the most popular of the aftermarket carburetors are the Model E and G "shorty" carburetors from S&S. These butterfly carburetors are designed to tuck in close to the engine and leave plenty of room for the rider's leg.

little extra gas down the carb throat when the guy in the Buick tries to pass on the right.

When trying to describe carburetors it seems there are as many exceptions as there are rules. So rather than continue describing a theoretical carburetor, it might be easier to start in with descriptions of the various types of carburetors and follow that up with a brief explanation of each of the most popular carburetors currently on the market.

Butterfly Carburetors

A fixed venturi carburetor, also known as a butterfly carburetor, has a fixed restriction in the throat. A "butterfly" valve is used to control the amount of air flowing through the carburetor throat. Fuel for high-speed operation is usually introduced at the venturi, while fuel for idle and low-speed operation is often introduced into the throat closer to the butterfly valve.

Supporters of this design cite the fact that butterfly carburetors have been used on everything from Model A Fords to Harley-David-

son motorcycles. In the aftermarket, the S&S, RevTech, Bendix, Screamin' Eagle, and several others are all butterfly designs.

Constant-Velocity and Slide Carburetors

Some carburetors vary the size of the venturi in the carburetor throat according to throttle position or engine load. These variable-venturi designs come in two basic models (more on these later). Usually the slide or variable restriction is connected to a tapered needle that passes through the main jet. In this way, increases in venturi size (and air flow) are tied directly to increases in fuel.

The two styles of variable-venturi carburetors are the constant-velocity design, which we often call a CV carburetor, and the straight variable-venturi design, sometimes called a slide carburetor.

In the CV design the throttle is connected to a conventional butterfly valve. Upstream from the butterfly valve is the variable restriction in the carburetor throat. This restriction is held in the closed position by a spring and opens according to the size of vacuum within the carb throat. More vacuum causes the piston to open farther, increasing the size of the venturi. At idle, for example, both the butterfly and the venturi are closed. As the throttle is opened more vacuum is applied to the slide piston, the piston moves up until equilibrium is achieved between the spring pushing down and the vacuum pulling up. As the slide or piston moves up, the tapered needle is pulled out of the jet, effectively increasing the size of the jet. The most common CV carburetors in the aftermarket are the SU and the billet carburetor from Carl's. The Keihin carb used on factory bikes since the late-1980s is also a CV design.

The non-CV carbs with variable venturi are usually known as

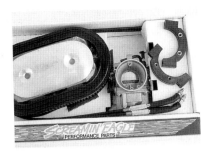

From Harley-Davidson comes another butterfly design, the Screamin' Eagle carburetor, which comes in this kit, complete with cables and a new air cleaner.

slide or smooth-bore carburetors. These designs eliminate the butterfly altogether and connect the throttle cable to the slide. The slide is connected to a tapered needle that passes through the main jet. As you open the throttle the slide opens the venturi, allowing more air through the carburetor throat. At the same time the tapered needle is raised in the jet, effectively increasing the size of the jet and adding more fuel to the increased air flow. Slide types of carburetors include the Mikuni and the QwikSilver 2.

Fans of the variable-venturi carburetors, both CV and slide type, point out the simplicity of the design. A design that eliminates most of the extra circuits needed with a fixed-venturi design and replaces them with one main jet and one tapered needle. Adherents of the CV carburetor design point out the fact that these carbs only open up to admit as much air as the engine can use under a particular load. You may open the throttle, but the piston will open only as far as needed. This keeps air speed through the carburetor high and aids throttle response.

Fans of the slide or smooth-bore designs like the fact that by eliminating the butterfly you eliminate a major obstruction in the carburetor

Shovelheads have become rather uncommon, and thus retain a certain allure. New Shovelheads can now be built or purchased based on new Shovelhead-style castings from S&S Cycle.

throat and create the "smooth bore," a bore that will pass more air (with less turbulence) for a given size than any other design.

Which Carb Is for You?

The number of aftermarket carburetors available for the V-twin engine is large and growing. Though a few are technically out of production, the SU for example, rebuilt models of those earlier designs are still available from reliable sources.

Whether your V-twin is mild or wild, there's a carburetor out there that's right for you—actually three or four carburetors. The trick here is to pick the one that's right for your application.

In choosing a carburetor, consider how it fits the bike. Will it interfere with your right leg? And what style of air cleaners will fit the carb? Some of the bigger carbs won't clear your 5-gallon Fat Bob tanks. Be sure when you buy the carb that you get the right style and length of throttle cables. If you want your carburetor in show chrome, note that some of the current aftermarket carburetors are available in polished or chrome-plated versions, while other manufacturers insist you *not* chrome-plate their carburetors.

The single most important thing to consider before buying the carburetor is how it will work in relation to your engine with your

particular combination of parts. If you have a good shop doing all or most of the work on your engine, consider the shop's suggestions before buying a new carburetor. Ask around to be sure the carb you want is easy to tune and that jets and other parts are readily available. Remember that bigger isn't always better and sometimes a carburetor that's too big results in low air velocity in the carburetor throat and poor low-speed response. This last comment is particularly true when considering some of the smooth-bore designs.

Because the emphasis of this book is street engines, some competition types of carburetors have been left out of the following product descriptions.

What's Out There

The Typhoon from Carl's

Carl's new "billet" carburetor is a CV design, the only carburetor manufactured from a solid chunk of 6061-T6 aluminum. Inside the shiny aluminum body you will find a large piston or "slide" with a tapered needle pressed in at the bottom of the piston. Like all carburetors of this type, engine vacuum, working against the spring, determines the position of the slide. The position of the slide, in turn, controls the amount of fuel that enters the airstream as the tapered needle is pulled farther and farther out of the main jet.

This new carburetor measures 50.8 mm in diameter (2 inches), big enough to feed the largest of motors. Yet this same carb works fine on a smaller 80-cubic-inch engine simply by changing the size of the tapered needle. The main jet can be adjusted externally without disassembling the carburetor, even while the bike is running, though if you ever do have to disassemble one of these you will find it to be very simple inside.

RevTech Accelerator II from Custom Chrome

Designed from the start for Custom Chrome, this butterfly-style carburetor features replaceable venturi-sleeves so the carburetor can grow with your engine. Venturi sleeves of 38, 42, and 45 mm are available to help this carburetor adapt to everything from an 80- to a 120-cubic-inch Big Twin.

Most butterfly carburetors have an accelerator pump, and this RevTech model features a high-volume pump designed to squirt the fuel into the center of the venturi for even distribution to the cylinders. Designed to operate with the current two-cable system, this carburetor has an enrichment device instead of a true choke. It allows the user to change both low- and high-speed gasoline jets and the high-speed air jet for complete tunability.

QwikSilver 2 from Edelbrock

From one of the largest automotive aftermarket parts suppliers comes the QwikSilver 2 carburetor. The QuikSilver 2 is a flat-slide, variable-venturi carburetor available in sizes ranging from 36 to 42 mm. All sizes are available in two mounting styles, flange-mount or grommet-mount.

Some interesting innovations exclusive to the QwikSilver include a single fuel circuit controlled by a single needle that is the same width from top to bottom with a tapered flat section cut out of the back side of the needle. As the air passes through the venturi past the needle, it creates a low-pressure area, which allows the fuel to move up the pickup tube and into the venturi. As the throttle is opened farther the needle moves out of the pickup tube, allowing more fuel to flow past the needle.

Another feature is the ability to self-compensate for altitude changes. The float bowl is vented to the venturi rather than to the atmosphere like most carburetors. By venting to the venturi, the float bowl is pressurized with the same pressure as air traveling through the venturi.

Because the QwikSilver does not have an accelerator pump, venturi size is critical when choosing the right size carburetor for your specific motor. The recommended venturi size is based on cubic inches according to the following chart.

Recommended sizes:

55 to 73 cubic inches	36 mm
74 to 84 cubic inches	38 mm
85 to 103 cubic inches	40 mm
104 cubic inches and larger	42 mm

Nitrous oxide injection is just one more way of adding oxygen because more oxygen (combined with more gas of course) means more power. Nitrous has two additional advantages. In Jekyl and Hyde fashion it allows you to run a mild streetable motor that turns into a wild machine at the push of a button. The bottle and hardware make for a bold visual "bad boy" statement that's hard to beat.

The SU Carburetor from Rivera

Originally designed for use on automobiles like the venerable MG and Triumph, the SU is a CV design that has long been used on V-twin motorcycles. Like most CV designs the SU has both a butterfly valve and a slide in the carburetor throat. At idle, the butterfly, connected to the throttle, is closed and the slide is positioned near the bottom of its travel. As the throttle is opened, engine vacuum works to pull the slide piston up, which, in turn, pulls the tapered needle farther out of the main jet, providing more fuel in direct proportion to the increased air flow.

The SU uses at least two interesting design details: A bimetallic support for the main jet, which provides automatic compensation for temperature change, and hydraulic damping of the slide piston, which keeps it from moving too far too fast.

Available from Rivera and Rivera dealers, the SU comes in kit form with the correct intake manifold and all necessary hardware, and is designed to work with dual-cable throttles.

Super E and G from S&S

The Super E and G carburetors from S&S are among the most popular of the many carburetors available for current Evo-style Big Twins. These two "shorty" carburetors are both butterfly designs measuring 1-7/8 inch (47.6 mm) for the E, and 2-1/16 inch (52.3 mm) for the G, measured at the throat. Compared to the earlier B model from S&S, these two carburetors are 1-7/16 inch shorter and designed to tuck neatly into the right side of the bike.

Features of the Super E and G include an easy-to-reach idle-mixture screw and changeable mid- and high-speed jets. Instead of a choke, an enrichment circuit is used. Attached to the air cleaner backing plate, the "choke" lever is located in a convenient position at the back edge of the air cleaner.

With two sizes available, the S&S Shorty carbs will work on everything from relatively small displacement V-twins to strokers and big-bore engines.

Screamin' Eagle Carburetor from Harley-Davidson

The Screamin' Eagle is a 40-mm butterfly-style carburetor designed for high airflow and increased horsepower throughout the rpm range. This carburetor from The Motor Company features an accelerator pump and three fully adjustable circuits. The Screamin' Eagle carbure-

Vance & Hines claims this two-into-one exhaust system for Sportsters will provide increased torque throughout the power band and boost horsepower up to 15 percent. *Drag Specialties*

tor is designed to operate with a two-cable throttle system and comes with a high-flow air cleaner.

Mikuni

Long known as the manufacturer of high-performance fuel-mixers, Mikuni offers three carburetors designed to work on an all-American V-twin. The company's 45- and 42-mm carburetors are intended for large-displacement and high-horsepower applications, while the 40-mm design is intended for milder 80-cubic-inch engines. All three Mikuni carbs feature a roller bearing slide assembly for precise movement and a light return spring.

Like other carburetors of this type, the Mikuni "smooth bores" have no butterfly in the throttle bore to restrict air flow at full throttle. This means that a 40-mm Mikuni will often flow more air than a larger carb of a different style.

The Mikuni carbs are designed for a dual-cable throttle cable, most Mikuni kits come complete

with their own cable set, which may be used with a standard throttle assembly.

A Final Note

All the manufacturers I talked to in assembling this section stressed the importance of properly matching the carburetor to the particular engine it will be used on. Be sure to read all the manufacturers' recommendations and call them before buying if you have lingering doubts. Try to purchase your carburetor from a reputable local shop, one that can help with tuning tips or parts you might need for the installation.

Buying from a good shop will minimize the tuning you need to do after the installation. If tuning is necessary, be sure to think first and swap jets second. If you do have trouble with that new carb, don't be afraid to ask a few questions, either from the shop where you bought it or from the technicians on the other end of the tech-line provided by most of the manufacturers.

Designed to enhance the performance of modified 80-cubic-inch engines, the Python II exhaust system combines high performance with the traditional look of staggered duals. This system uses an anti-reversion cone in each pipe and a muffler baffle intended to provide a distinctive exhaust note. *Drag Specialties*

Camshafts and Valve Gear

Before trying to discuss how to choose the right camshaft, it might be helpful to discuss the basics of camshaft operation and the terms used to describe each camshaft.

At the risk of being too simple, it might be instructive to first consider each of the four strokes and how the camshaft affects and is affected by the power, exhaust, intake, and compression strokes. Because the camshaft runs at half the speed of the crankshaft, the camshaft will turn one complete revolution to the crankshaft's two. Remember, too, that most cam specifications are given in degrees of *crankshaft* rotation. Also, the cam in a V-twin runs backwards from engine rotation, which confuses people.

Power Stroke

On the beginning of the power stroke, with the piston approaching top dead center (TDC), both valves are closed. A spark causes pressure in the cylinder to build, forcing the piston down in the cylinder. As the piston nears bottom dead center (BDC), the pressure, and power production, drop off. In order to get as much of the spent gas out of the cylinder as possible the exhaust valve opens before the piston actually reaches BDC. With a typical mild street camshaft the exhaust valve opens at about 60 (crankshaft degrees) before the piston hits BDC.

Exhaust Stroke

The exhaust valve is open as this stroke begins, and stays open during the entire 180 degrees of the exhaust stroke. In order to pack as much fresh gas as possible into the cylinder, especially during higher rpm, the intake valve opens before the piston hits TDC. This period when both valves are open is known as the overlap period, during this time the outgoing exhaust gasses help to draw the intake charge in behind them. Typical street cams begin opening the intake valve at about 30 degrees before the piston reaches TDC during the exhaust stroke.

Intake Stroke

As the intake stroke begins, both valves are open. By about 25 degrees past TDC, the exhaust valve has closed, ending the overlap period. The intake valve remains open during the rest of the intake stroke.

Puff the Magic Dragon is alive and well in the form of this Turbo kit from Aerocharger. Adjustable vanes are said to eliminate any turbo-lag while bearings with their own oil supply minimize plumbing and lubrication hassles. Run 8 psi on stock engines or more on modified mills. As this kit proves, there's more than one way to get extra power from that V-twin engine.

Compression Stroke

Though it would seem best to close the intake valve when the piston hits BDC, the gas and air are coming into the cylinder with a certain momentum (especially at higher rpm) and the piston doesn't really start to build pressure until it has traveled partway up into the cylinder. For these reasons the intake valve stays open into the early part of the compression stroke. A typical street cam closes the intake valve at about 40 degrees after BDC.

Harley-Davidson makes a variety of camshafts under the Screamin' Eagle name. Some of the milder designs allow you to retain the stock pushrods, while the more aggressive grinds require that you use adjustable pushrods.

Which Camshaft Is Right For You?

Before choosing a camshaft, consider the wise words written in the Andrews Camshaft catalog regarding the choice of a cam: "There are no hard and fast rules for picking a cam for a specific application. However, some basic guidelines are worth talking about.

Most performance cams are chosen for the elementary purpose of producing more power. It is important to remember that too much cam sometimes results in a reduction in power, not the increase that was expected.

Generally, engines that are to be run on the street will perform better with a milder increase in lift and duration than more radical grinds. While bigger cams may have a higher peak output (at high rpm), a milder cam may feel much better to a street rider where some low rpm power is important. The message is, if in doubt, play it conservatively. . . ."

Ignition

Modern Harley-Davidsons have replaced the ignition points with a "hall effect" or magnetic sensor. The sensor is in turn connected to the ignition module. The module is used to actually control the voltage to the coil and the timing of the spark. Factory modules have two curves, a faster curve for optimum conditions and a slower (or retarded) curve with less advance to minimize pinging under heavy load conditions. Which one the module uses depends on whether or not the VOES (vacuum-operated electrical switch) is open or closed. This VOES is normally open under acceleration and conditions of low vacuum and closed during idle and cruise, or high-vacuum, conditions.

Aftermarket Systems

Differences in the available aftermarket ignition systems include the type of sensor used to provide timing information, whether or not the system uses a module, how it controls the ignition advance, and whether or not a VOES switch is used. You can retain the factory pickup and simply replace the stock module with one that provides a faster advance curve, or a curve that can be tailored to suit your needs and riding style. Some of these modules use the VOES switch, while others do not.

Other aftermarket ignition systems are more complete and replace both the sensor and the module. The advance curve on these ignitions may be controlled mechanically with weights or controlled electronically within the self-contained ignition system.

Single and Dual Fire

Factory ignition systems and many aftermarket ignitions operate in what is known as dual-fire mode. That is, the coil fires both spark plugs at the same time. Stated another way, when one cylinder is near TDC on the compression stroke and ready for the power stroke, the plug on that cylinder fires; at the same time the other cylinder also fires. The spark in the "other" cylinder is known as the wasted spark. Specifically, when the front cylinder fires, the rear cylinder is at 10 degrees after TDC; and when the rear cylinder fires, the front cylinder is at 80 degrees before TDC. These figures assume 35 degrees timing advance.

In theory, it would be more efficient to fire each plug alone, called single fire, and the more sophisticated ignitions do exactly that. When the front cylinder comes up to TDC that spark plug, and only that spark plug, fires. Though before-and-after dyno

Total horsepower, and where that horsepower occurs in the rpm range, are both affected by the camshaft timing. Crane Hi-Roller camshafts allow the engine builder to install the camshaft straight up, or 4 degrees advanced or retarded. A wide range of grinds are available to suit nearly any engine-building project. *Custom Chrome*

tests show little or no direct increase in horsepower, the switch to single-fire ignition seems to result in a smoother running engine as judged by seat-of-the-pants testing.

If you are upgrading the ignition, you can simply install a different module, or a complete system, complete with sensor and coils for single-fire usage. Ignition changes should be made in concert with the other changes you are making to the engine, and if a certain mechanic is doing the work on the bike, rely on that person's advice for your new ignition.

Some mechanics like to use the factory pickup and either a factory or aftermarket module simply because the parts have been proven reliable. And if there is any trouble, replacement parts can be found at any dealership and many independent shops.

Before you buy anything, remember that electronic ignitions put out more power, more reliably,

You can upgrade the ignition with a new module, like the Dyna 2000, or a complete system like the H1-4.

than any points type of system. Despite the allure of "simpler" and older systems, the hot ticket is an electronic ignition with electronic control of the advance. Which one you buy will depend on your budget and your engine. More compression requires more spark to jump the same gap. Getting enough spark means a reliable pickup, the right module (if your system uses one), a coil with enough output in kilovolts, and quality wires that will deliver that output to the plugs without any danger of leakage or crossfire.

A Computerized Crystal Ball: The Craig Walters Accelerator Program

Until recently it was pretty tough to predict the exact outcome of a given combination of parts—unless the combination was one an engine builder had already used. And a package of parts that worked well in an 80-cubic-inch engine with 10:1 compression might not work so well with an 89-cubic-inch engine with 9:1 compression.

Wouldn't it be nice if you or I could start off with the basic engine we think we need and then experiment on paper with the dif-

ferent camshafts, carburetors, and compression ratios? Instead of gambling that some new cam profile from Andrews or Sifton will work with the rest of the engine we could "dyno" the engine—with that new camshaft—on paper.

Well, due to the wonders of technology anyone with a decent computer and the right software can do exactly that. The Accelerator software, developed by Craig Walters (who does a great deal of head and camshaft development for the aftermarket) provides a means to predict the outcome, in terms of horsepower and torque, of various engine combinations.

As with any other tool the outcome or success of this software is dependent on the skill of the operator. When computers were new there was a popular phrase, "garbage in, garbage out." That pretty well sums up the idea that the computer can only process the information it is provided. The Walters software is no different. Though it's not terribly complex, it does work best in the right hands.

The program has inputs for all the standard engine parameters like bore, stroke, and rod length. By inserting the combustion chamber volume, or a known compression ratio, the program will give you either a standard or a corrected compression ratio (the corrected ratio takes into account the effect of the camshaft on the compression ratio the engine actually sees). The static compression figure this software provides is a good indicator of possible starting troubles if it's too high.

An important input is that of the cubic-feet-per minute (cfm) measurement that the heads will flow. In this way, an engine builder can measure the exact effect of a good porting job on engine output.

When you're upgrading the engine to produce more power, you need to upgrade the ignition as well. Heavy-duty coils like this provide a higher output yet are compatible with stock 1984 and later electronic ignitions. *Custom Chrome*

In addition to predicting horsepower and torque throughout the rpm range, the program gives a prediction of volumetric efficiency and also provides piston velocity. The piston velocity, given at both an average and maximum figure, is a good way to predict future troubles with stroker motors.

Some of the information is generated on the screen and is not part of the printout—the cam warning screen, for example, which provides specific warnings if the cam choice is way off the mark.

This program will also predict elapsed times and trap speed at the drag strip. The Walters' software is also a good tool for a shop, a great way to show customers what they're likely to get from a particular part and in some cases convince them to use parts that are different than those they originally had in mind.

For more information, contact Mid-USA or ask around at the local shops that already have this software.

ENGINE BUILDERS SPEAK OUT

Everybody wants a little extra power. You can blame it on the EPA, and say the stock bikes are strangled for power. Or you can put the whole thing on the Harley engineers for refusing to unleash the potential lurking in those stock factory cases and cylinders. Maybe you can admit that you simply want to go faster and kick butt on the guy next door. Whatever the reason, more power is like good sex: We all want it. And like sex, we all brag in public that we've got it. In the privacy of our own garage, however, we wonder if all that money we spent with the mail-order firms was really worthwhile.

There is an entire segment of the after-market dedicated to selling components that will make your bike fast (or at least, faster). Claims and counterclaims abound. Each new carburetor that comes out spawns a whole series of tech articles, each with its own before-and-after dyno chart.

In an effort to shed some light on this subject, I've interviewed two mechanics, Tim Wolff and Lee Clemens, who have an abundance of experience working on V-twins. Though Wolff works in a dealership and Clemens in a well-known independent shop, each has a valid viewpoint. Both Wolff and Clemens make their living by helping Harley riders go faster and each lives in the real world, where if the bike doesn't run better when they're done, the customer raises hell and gets his or her money back.

I've asked each mechanic a similar set of questions. Some are philosophical in nature, and intended to make you think, whereas others are more specific, intended to help you decide what to buy. When reading this section remember two things: Just as there are a variety of recipes for apple pie, all of them good, there is more than one group of parts and procedures that will provide a given level of performance for a V-twin. And though a chassis dyno is a great tool, not all dynos are calibrated the same or run "by the book."

Unless noted otherwise, all comments refer to 80 cubic inch Evolution Big Twin and Evolution Sportsters, both 883 and 1200 cc.

Tim Wolff, St. Paul Harley-Davidson

Tim Wolff is a mechanic at St. Paul Harley-Davidson, located just east of St. Paul, Minnesota. Wolff got his training at MMI and the factory, and has been wrenching on Harleys for nearly five years, including two years at St. Paul.

Q *What are the mistakes people make when they hop up their Harley-Davidsons?*

A One of them is to buy something they don't need. They overcarburate the bikes. A motor will only breathe so much, but they put this humongous carb on there which slows down the breathing ability of the motor. The really big carburetor lowers the velocity of the air coming in. People always want to throw out the stock carb and install a Mikuni or S&S instead. Most of the time, unless you're going to get really radical, it's not necessary to replace the stock CV carb.

Tim Wolff is a factory trained mechanic from St. Paul Harley-Davidson.

That's probably the biggest mistake people make. Right away they buy all these extra components that don't really add to the performance level. They just add to the price. Another mistake is exhaust pipes. The stock ones perform pretty well if you take the baffles out. Lots of times riders spend $500 and all they get is an extra set of exhaust pipes lying around their garage.

 Other mistakes?

 Mismatching components. A guy says, "I'm going to get Porker pipes because I like the way they look," and he doesn't consider the other components on the engine. You've got to look at the complete package. You don't bolt on just a carburetor or just an exhaust system. You have to make sure everything goes together so they don't detract from each other. And again you save yourself some money this way. You don't want to get all done and say, "Well, I'd like to go a little bit faster, so now I have to install a different camshaft."

Unreasonable expectations are another problem. They'll say, "I want my FLHS to beat my buddy's Ninja off the line." Well, it probably could do it, but you'd have quite a Frankenstein on your hands. Who knows how many millions it would cost? You have a bike designed to do a certain thing, and one of its big benefits is that it's malleable, but some people expect a little bit more out of it than it has to offer.

 So what's a better way to get extra power without wasting a lot of money?

 Decide first how you're going to use the bike; think about exactly

what you want. If you can, nail down exactly what you need, like, "I want to have twice the mid-range torque that I have now," that's better. Nail down exactly what parameters you want, then say, "What do I need to achieve this?" Sometimes looks are important. If you have to have Bad Company pipes, then maybe you have to change some of the other components to make good use of those pipes. If you've got to have a certain Mikuni carburetor, ask yourself what else do you need to have to make that an effective piece? You have to know what you want. A lot of people don't know what they want. They just read through the magazines and see a few neat bikes and say, "Yeah. That'd be neat." They haven't really sat down and considered it really carefully.

Before starting on the project, these riders need to know how they ride and where they want the extra power—are they looking for top end or mid-range? Or do they want to pull really hard right off the line?

Once you know exactly what you're looking for in terms of power, you need to determine which combination of parts will get you there. Understand too that more than one combination may work. It comes back to knowing what you want, and what to do to get it.

 What would some of your favorite combinations be for a fairly mild 80-cubic-inch Evo, a bike that gets used on the street and maintains good longevity and reasonable mileage?

 It depends on what the customer wants to spend. The biggest rule of the game is how big is your pocketbook at the time you want to do something. A good low-dollar package is a little bolt-in cam (the Screamin' Eagle bolt-in cam), a Screamin'

Eagle air cleaner, and the stock pipes opened up. That's a very popular package at our shop. It's got good longevity. You can tune the Keihin carburetor pretty well compared to the way it comes off the storeroom floor. That's an excellent package that's relatively cheap, and everybody who gets it either says, "I'm totally satisfied," or they might say, "I like it but I have to have a little more."

 If they have to have more, then what's the next step?

The next step, especially if you want more mid-range torque, is to jack the compression up. There are a lot of different ways to do that. One we really like to do is with a set of Wiseco pistons. They're a good, high-quality piston. Those pistons are a little bigger than stock, so we like to hone out the cylinder an additional 0.005 inches; that way we know the cylinder is perfectly straight and round. These pistons raise the compression without modifying the head or changing the combustion chamber shape. Those are quick and easy to put in; I've never had any negative feedback on that combination. Nothing but praise from our customers.

Why would you rather use the piston and not shave the head?

Once you start milling that head there's all kinds of ideas of how much you're going to mill off and the possible changes to the combustion chamber shape. And if the owner wants to put a different cam in the bike with more lift, then you're talking piston and valve clearance problems. The Wiseco pistons come with nice, deep valve pockets. You can get pretty radical in the cams with little clearance problems. Yes, you can mill the head, but you just have to be a lot more careful. A lot more measuring and more time. Does the customer have an interest in paying for all that? We kind of reserve milling the head for when the customer wants to get really extreme.

 What's a combination you guys use, or see a lot, that you like?

We've got a number of engines out with Jerry Branch heads, or we do the head work here. We clean up the ports a little bit and do a good valve job, add the Wiseco pistons, get a cam selected for the compression ratio, and we can get 90 horses, no problem. Depending on the kind of carburetor and pipes you put on, you can get thousands of miles on those high-performance engines with no longevity problem. No pinging. You don't have to run 110-octane fuel or anything in there. You do need to pick a cam that's got enough overlap so it blows a lot of the compression out. You end up with a good strong-running high-compression engine. We've had a lot of happy customers with that setup, too.

 So you've got to match the cam with the compression?

Absolutely. Otherwise, you could end up with a real short-lived beast after they kick the compression way up. We've run into that problem. With high compression you want a cam that has a fairly good sized overlap so you can get it started with a regular starter. Otherwise you might have a "grunter" that will sit there and click and that's all.

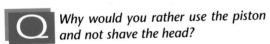 **What about the Sportsters? Is an increase in the displacement, from 883 to 1200cc, a good horsepower-per-dollar deal?**

Yes. That's a good start. They have an 883 and they drive them around, and they go, "Wow, this is just a super pooch. My car is faster than this." Then they put the 1200 kit in it and the Screamin' Eagle cams and they go, "Holy cow, it's twice as fast as it used to be." And it probably is. And that's usually enough for them. It's quick and easy and gives good results.

Lee Clemens at Departure Bike Works

When I asked Lee Clemens, owner of Departure Bike Works in Richmond, Virginia, how long he's been working on Harleys he had to stop and think for a minute. "Well, I've been working on bikes as far back as I can remember. There was a Triumph Cub I had as a kid—I must have been 10 or 12 at the time—so I guess I've been working on these things for nearly 40 years."

Clemens started his drag racing career in the early 1970s with the dirt drags. "But then we got tired of the dirt so we started running at the regular quarter-mile tracks in the area. I remember we took a rigid frame, added a new rear section, and then used an XLCR tank to give it a little style. We put a 98 cubic inch Big Twin engine in that thing and we did pretty well. But I also remember it was a pretty stiff learning curve, 'cause, boy, I blew up my share of motors. You really learn what works, what doesn't, and why."

Today, Clemens is running a Pro Stock bike and getting ready to celebrate Departure's 25th anniversary. Twenty-five years of building street bikes by day and race bikes by night means he has seen both the mistakes people make and the victories they achieve when modifying a V-twin engine to extract extra power.

Q *What are the biggest mistakes people make when they set out to get more power from their street bikes?*

A The biggest is not sitting down and planning out what they're going to do. If you're building a house or whatever you have to start with a plan. But people look at a motor, they just decide that they want more power and jump into it. First, if they have no knowledge at all, they need to get a couple of books—car or bike books that cover the basics of hopping up an engine. Better yet, they should find someone they trust and tell that person what they want to do. They have to be specific about this. I see guys come in the shop and they aren't asking questions; they're buy-ing parts. They get a cam that doesn't come on until 3500 rpm even though most of their riding is done at only 3500 rpm. So it's the wrong cam for the application. I think Harley riders have this attitude that if big is good, bigger is better and too much is just right.

Q *How should people go about this hop-up business so they avoid those mistakes?*

A Avoid the mistakes through planning. Ask yourself, "What am I going to do with this bike?" If they do mostly short hops in town, tell that to the guy who's building the motor. You need to know what rpm you're riding at so the person building the engine can make it work at that speed.

Each piece of the performance package—the carb, cam, exhaust pipes, and heads—is extremely critical; they have to be looked at as one mass. You have to consider them together because each one affects the others.

Q *Do you want to talk about one or two combinations that you like, that make good power on a street bike?*

A With the stock Evo, especially 1996 and later, the heads seem pretty good; they lend themselves to good horsepower. The earlier heads might need a mild amount of porting work. If someone *is* going to get in there and work on the heads, then I like to see them install at least a good exhaust valve, because a good stainless valve from Manley or Baisley will last a long time. And if they install a good intake valve it will improve the flow.

For a camshaft, the 1-1100 from Crane is a good cam and there shouldn't be any clearance problems except with the real early Evo engines, like '84 and '85, which have no cutouts for the valves. If they're changing the cam, they have to install a set of adjustable push rods at the same time.

For the carburetor I recommend the S&S E series. It's a simple carb to work on, and if you have trouble everybody has parts for an S&S. You can, however, make a step up to a slightly better carb, the HSR 42. The Mikuni works well with a mild or a more heavily tweaked 80-cubic-inch motor. It's a little more complex but it makes good horsepower.

For power on the street the Thunder header is the best deal I've seen. The Super-Trapp two-into-one is also very good, and it has the advantage of being tunable.

For riders who really need to have a more traditional exhaust, the Python system is O.K. Some of the new ones from Vance & Hines are selling well and are reported to be good too, but I haven't tried them on the dyno yet. People should remember that the Evo motor does not like a straight pipe. If you've got to have straights, then at least use an AR (anti-reversion) type of pipe.

For ignition I like the new Crane HI 4, because it allows you to add a few degrees of timing to that back cylinder, which the motors always seem to like. The Compu-fire is a good one, too.

With this combination we usually see 75 to 80 horses at the rear wheel with an equal amount of torque on our dyno. The stock bikes run 52 to 54 horsepower. To some people this may not sound like a lot of horsepower; however, with the amount of torque you gain plus the placement of the horsepower (in the mid-range), this is a very strong setup.

Q *How do you feel about using the Keihin CV carburetor, the one the factory's been using since the late 1980s?*

A I think the CV is fine on milder engines, though I do think the bikes run much better if the Keihin carb is equipped with the new Dyna Jet Thunderslide kit.

Q *What about the jaded individual who wants even more power than is available with the first combinations you mentioned?*

A A second combination I like uses the Axtell wedge pistons [note: use of the Axtell pistons requires machining the stock combustion chamber]. These are one of the best ways to bump compression and keep an excellent combustion chamber shape. The wedge pistons push the compression up to 10:1, but the combustion chamber shape helps hold down heat so detonation is not a problem. This piston, along with a Crane 1-1102 cam, an S&S E or Mikuni HSR-42 carburetor, Crane HI 4 ignition and a good set of pipes should net out at 80 to 90 horsepower—depending on the amount of head work. That's rear wheel horsepower measured on the dyno, with approximately the same amount of torque. Again, I feel this is a very strong combination because of horsepower placement and lots of torque.

Q *What about Sportsters?*

A The 1200 Sportster motor is an excellent motor. It lends itself very nicely to added horsepower. I also feel the 883 to 1200 conversion is a very good way to go—we use the Wiseco pistons for this because they are offered in two versions (flat-top or dished) and they are superior quality. The 883 heads are different for '86 and '87 (the first two years of production). They have a small bathtub chamber of approximately 50 cc and would require the dished pistons unless the chambers are reworked completely.

We use the Baisley valves for the 883 conversion because they will flow as much as a larger valve without actually going to the large valve; therefore we do not have to replace the valve seat to accommodate a bigger valve. Harley's Screamin' Eagle cams seem to be a good cam set for the Sportster engine. One set that they offer does not even require adjustable pushrods.

We have found the newer ('92 and up) XL cases are slightly harder to work with if we use larger cam profiles because of the cast-in lifter housings. In some cases the cam lobes are running into the lower part of the tappet guide hole.

We do feel the XL motors offer a better pushrod approach [less deflection of the pushrods] than the Big Twin motor. This translates into better control of the valve train.

Lee Clemens has been building radical vee-twin drag bikes since the early 1970s. Clemens' Departure Bike Works campaigned this beast in the Pro Stock class in 1997. It posted a best time of 8.70 seconds at 150 miles per hour. *Photo courtesy Departure Bike Works*

ST. PAUL HARLEY-DAVIDSON ADDS REAL-WORLD POWER

There are as many ways to get extra power from your Harley-Davidson as there are manufacturers of aftermarket parts. This section documents real-world improvements made to two engines.

At St. Paul Harley-Davidson, a Big Twin is massaged for more horsepower while retaining the basic dependability and low-rpm grunt that modern Evolution engines are known for. The work at St. Paul includes new pistons, camshaft, and mufflers. The second case study documents the enlargement of a Sportster from 883 to 1200cc in the garage of Don Hand, building contractor by day and Harley enthusiast by night.

So follow along as a group of experienced mechanics use two very different means of extracting additional power from two very different Harley-Davidson engines.

1 After pulling off the gas tank and carb, Tim Wolff removes the rocker boxes. Then the pushrods come out, followed by the cylinder heads.

St. Paul Harley-Davidson is located just east of downtown St. Paul, Minnesota, and is equipped with a Dyno Jet chassis dyno and a group of technicians familiar with its operation. Before tear-down, the bike in question is run on the dyno to get a good "before" reading.

The standard dyno run at St. Paul is a roll-on test done to check for maximum horsepower and torque. Tim Wolff, the technician, starts the test by warming up the bike, running it up through the gears, and then doing the actual test in forth gear. With one eye on the tachometer that's part of the dyno, Wolff does the roll-on test, running the bike up close to the red line. The Dyno Jet screen shows the horse-

power and torque figures during the run and then prints out a graph when the dyno run is finished.

The result in this case is very close to the output figures obtained with most stock, late-model Evos. "50 to 52 horsepower is pretty standard," explains Wolff. "A looser engine with more miles on it may go to 54 or 55 horsepower."

Wolff goes on to explain that the owner of this stock 1993 FLHS, "wants more torque and isn't so worried about the horsepower figures we get afterward. I think that's pretty intelligent because most riders don't ride at the point where the engine gets peak horses, but they do spend a lot of time riding close to the torque peak."

The package St. Paul Harley-Davidson is installing in the 80-

cubic-inch Evo is one they've used before. It's a combination of relatively mild components that provide a good increase in mid-range torque. The camshaft is a Screamin' Eagle bolt-in cam (note, there are three "bolt-in" Screamin' Eagle cams; this is the mildest of the three). Because this is a mild cam, there is no need to check for valve-to-piston clearance or to install adjustable pushrods. For a boost in compression, St. Paul likes to install a set of Wiseco pistons with an advertised static compression figure of 10:1. The boys at St. Paul recommend leaving on the stock Keihin CV carburetor instead of automatically replacing it with something bigger and faster.

To provide the carb with more air, the combination of parts includes a Screamin' Eagle air cleaner. Wolff likes the Screamin' Eagle air cleaner because it passes just as much air as anything else on the market, yet it's much less expensive than most aftermarket air cleaners.

To help the engine breathe easier on the other end, the stock bagger mufflers will be replaced with slip-fit "touring" mufflers from Harley-Davidson with the baffles removed. (Note, these mufflers are being redesigned as we go to press; the redesigned muffler may not make it so easy to remove the baffles.) Wolff explains that you could also use the SuperTrapp Dresser muffler or the HP Plus mufflers from Drag Specialties.

When I ask Wolff if it's necessary to port the factory heads, he explains that, "With the 80-cubic-inch engine there's a threshold of about 80 horsepower. Getting an 80-cube Evo to about 80 horses isn't too tough or too expensive. You can use a fairly mild cam, keep the stock carb and the stock heads. Going beyond that 80-horse level means you have to do more work and spend more money. Now you need a bigger carb, wilder cam, and maybe some porting work on the heads."

Disassembly

Wolff works on V-twins all day, every day, and the big FL engine comes apart quickly and easily. Once the tank is out of the way the carb and intake come off next. Wolff leaves the cables attached to the carb and ties it out of the way with a bungee cord. Once the intake manifold is off he shows me how the large rubber O-rings at each end of the intake have become hard and non-compliant. A close look shows that the rear gasket wasn't sealing, causing a vacuum leak on that cylinder.

2 After the heads are off, Wolff pulls the cylinders and will then put rags in the crankcase openings under the pistons to keep foreign material out of the crankcases. Once the cylinders are off, the circlips are removed and the pistons can be separated from the connecting rods.

4 This is the Jim's Machine tool, which can be used to replace the inner camshaft bearing, and the two bearings; the Torrington bearing with the additional rollers is on the left.

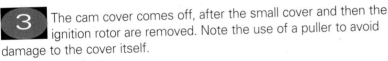

3 The cam cover comes off, after the small cover and then the ignition rotor are removed. Note the use of a puller to avoid damage to the cover itself.

With the top section of the rocker box off, Wolff loosens the four rocker support bolts and then the outer base bolts and then takes the whole rocker box assembly up off the heads. With the rocker boxes off the engine, Wolff pulls the pushrods out and sets them aside on the bench. (Note, it's a good idea to mark all the parts that come off the engine so they go back exactly where they came out).

Next he unscrews the head bolts, lifts the heads off partway, and pulls out the push rod tubes. At this point Wolff adds the comment that, "If you're just putting in base gaskets you can just slip the cylinder up far enough to slip out the wrist pin and thus keep the pistons, rings, and cylinders as an assembly."

But we're doing more than just base gaskets here, so after the heads are off Wolff pulls the cylin-ders off. Next he takes out the circlips, then the wrist pins, and finally the pistons. All this is done with the pistons near the top of their travel.

With the cylinders and pistons off it's time to disassemble the gear case. First Wolff drills out rivets on the cam cover and pulls the cover plate. Then he removes the pickup plate and the ignition rotor, which is screwed to the end of the cam. The bolts for the gear-case cover are next, but first Wolff sets a pan under the engine to catch the escaping oil. It's important to use a puller to remove the gear-case cover and not pry it off with screwdrivers.

With the cover off, Wolff removes the cam and breather gear and checks both for wear. The bore for the breather gear should be checked, too, as debris in the engine can become imbedded into the gear and then act like a cutting tool on the gear's bore.

Now Wolff pulls the tappet blocks and checks the lifter assemblies for wear. He starts by carefully cleaning all the oil out of the rollers and bearings. With no oil in the bearings Wolff tries to move the roller up and down (90 degrees to the roller axle). There should be no up and down play; if there is, then the lifter will be replaced as an assembly. This is because Harley-Davidson does not make repair kits for Evo lifters and also because the complete lifter assembly is priced very reasonably.

Note: At least one of my mechanic proofreaders made the comment that: "Unless the tappet rollers were very low mileage I would replace them with the cam so they would both have the same life expectancy."

With the heads and cylinders removed it's easy to check the cylinder studs to be sure they're tight in the crankcase. Wolff puts a stud

5 This shot shows the special driver used to install the inner cam bearing.

6 This is the new camshaft, with the thrust washer on the far right, and shim used to set the end play seen between the end of the cam and the thrust washer.

7 Here we see the cam installed for the first trial fitting; the light is illuminating the area where high-lift cams sometimes run into the factory case.

puller on each stud (this is for engines assembled before mid-1994 when the studs changed to a new design with the shoulder at the bottom). If a stud comes loose easily, with less than 10 pounds of torque, Wolff pulls that one and replaces it with a new style stud. If they don't want to come out easily he leaves them in, rather than risk galling the threads in the case. As Wolff explains, "There's nothing wrong with replacing only half the studs; they don't all have to match."

One of the last disassembly procedures is to remove the inner cam bearing. At St. Paul the technicians replace the inner cam bearing with the earlier style Torrington bearing (as opposed to the late-model stock roller bearing) whenever a high-lift camshaft is installed. A blind-hole puller and slide hammer are used to remove the inner

bearing. (Note: Jim's Machine makes a very good tool for this job.)

With the bearing out you can see the inner lip that the new bearing must seat up against. Wolff uses the correct tool and drives on the "numbers" side of the new bearing. It doesn't take much force, and after the bearing is seated he puts just a little oil on the rollers as a pre-lube.

Note: Before installing a new camshaft it's a good idea to make sure there's enough clearance between the innermost cam lobe and the case. High-lift cams may contact the case unless you do a little clearancing first.

Set Up the New Camshaft

Now it's time to set up and install the new camshaft. First, a word about specifications. Though the service manuals give the camshaft end-play specification as 0.001 to 0.050 inch, Wolff likes to see the end play in the 0.008- to 0.010-inch range. The end play is adjusted by using a thicker or thinner washer between the camshaft and the thrust plate. In order to get everything right, one or more trial

fittings are usually required. In this case Wolff assembled the gear case with the new Screamin' Eagle camshaft along with the stock thrust plate and a shim that measured 0.065 inch thick. From past experience Wolff knows the 0.065-inch shim often works well with the Screamin' Eagle camshaft; when it's a camshaft of unknown dimension, he starts with a 0.050-inch shim instead. Before bolting on the gear-case cover for the first trail fitting, the outer cam seal is removed. Now it's time to install the gear case with a pre-crushed gasket,

With the cam installed it's necessary to check both for gear fitment between the camshaft and pinion gear, and the end play of the camshaft. Though service manuals

ENGINE CASE STUDIES

NO SUBSTITUTE FOR CUBIC INCHES

This second sequence documents the transformation of a 1990 Sportster from 883 to 1200 cc. The bike is owned by Barb Sherwood of Ramsey, Minnesota. Most of the disassembly is performed by Sherwood's significant other, Don Hand, with help from Jason Mitchell. The reassembly, however, is the work of "Bug," a Harley-Davidson mechanic for 17 years and an employee of Kokesh MC Parts in Spring Lake Park, Minnesota.

Disassembly

First the battery is unhooked, which helps prevent any un-wanted arc welding during the disassembly process. Next, the bolts that hold the bars and headlight to the bike are removed, though the bars themselves are left strapped to the bike.

The seat is removed next, followed by the gas tank. Note: Sherwood's Sportster carries an FXRS tank, modified to fit the Sporty, and this is why the handlebars had

1 The bike in question is a 1990 Sportster. Though the engine is stock, Barb's Sporty does carry the FXR gas tank and flared rear fender. Because of the tank/bars combination, the handlebars must be moved out of the way before the gas tank can be removed. After the tank is removed, the ignition switch and bracket, coil, and exhaust pipes come off next. If possible, parts are simply unbolted and left wired to the bike to make reassembly easier.

to be moved out of the way. To make the tank fit, Hand had a new mounting tab welded onto the back, and then modified the front mount to better fit the "top tube" just behind the steering neck.

Sherwood's Cycle-Shack pipes come off next, followed by the choke bracket and then the carburetor—which like the bars is left with cables attached and held out of the way with a bungee cord.

The front motor mount attaches to the front head, so it needs to be removed. The coil, mounted under the tank, is unbolted but left wired to the bike.

Now starts the true engine work. Hand and Mitchell make quick work of removing the rocker box covers, the head bolts, and then the pushrods. Once the pushrods are out of the way, the heads can be removed and then the pushrod tubes. It's worth noting here that all the parts should be marked as they come off, so they go back on exactly where they came off.

After the heads are off, Hand holds down both cylinders while turning the engine over with the rear wheel (which is off the ground). Now he can pull off the cylinders and then stuff rags into the open crankcase under each piston so nothing can fall in while the engine is disassembled.

In the case of Sherwood's bike, the decision is made to pull off the right side engine cover, the lifter blocks, and the primary cover and send them out for powder coating. More complex than it sounds, pulling the cam cover means first drilling out the rivets and then removing the ignition cover. With the cover off, Hand takes out the screws that hold down the base plate and then the 3/16-inch bolt

2 With the carburetor and rocker boxes already removed it's time to take off the heads and cylinders. Note that as soon as the cylinder is up far enough, a clean rag is stuffed into the opening below the piston so debris and chunks of old gasket don't end up in the crankcase.

(5/16-inch head) that holds the ignition rotor on. Once the bolts holding the cover itself are removed, Hand can ease off the cover. This involves trying to pull the cover without having the camshafts drop out at the same time. The wiring for the ignition wraps up behind the starter and must be traced back and unplugged. As the cover comes off, Hand reaches in and disconnects the vent hose, which runs from the back of the cover to the oil tank.

Though the cylinders are honed to final size by Bug, the actual boring is done at Faribault Harley-Davidson in Faribault, Minnesota. The fitting and measuring methods can vary slightly from one piston manufacturer to another, and Bug fits the pistons per the instructions that came with the new Wiseco pistons.

Reassembly

The actual assembly starts with cleaning, as Bug carefully washes out the cylinders with soap and hot water, explaining as he does that, "the soap and water will remove the last of the honing residue better than solvent will." The new Wiseco pistons are designed with a reverse dome and will provide a 9.5:1 compression ratio (stock was 9:1). The new pistons with the concave top eliminate the need to remove material from the stock 883 combustion chamber, as is often done as part of a 1200 conversion when flat-top pistons are used.

As he gets ready to install the rings, Bug points out that the new pistons have a front and back, so it's necessary to read and follow the instructions. Likewise the rings, which have a top and bot-

3 Pulling the cam cover must be done carefully to avoid having the camshafts drop out of place. The ignition wiring from the pickup runs behind the starter to a connector, which must be located and disconnected before the cover can be completely removed.

4 Though the old pistons have a flat-top, the new pistons from Wiseco have a reverse-dome. Without the concave piston top, the combination of increased displacement and small combustion chamber can create a 12:1 combustion ratio.

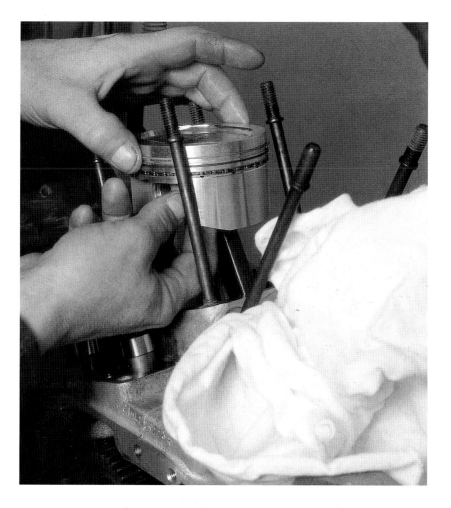

5 The cylinders have been bored out and final-honed to match the piston diameters. New piston rings are installed according to the manufacturer's directions, and then the pistons are installed on the connecting rods with new circlips on each side.

tom. Bug reports that when in doubt about a set of rings, "I always install them so the markings on the rings face up."

The pistons are installed on the connecting rods with new circlips on either side (never use the old ones). Bug sets the circlips in place so the opening doesn't line up with the gap in the piston. After installing the pistons, Bug lightly oils the pistons and the inside of the cylinders.

Next, he sets a plastic-handled pliers under the piston (this will hold the piston in place as the cylinder is pushed down), and then lowers the newly bored cylinder down over the rings while he compresses the rings with a ring compressor. Rather than drop the base gaskets onto the case before the cylinders are lowered into place, Bug prefers to stick them to the bottom of the cylinders with Gasgacinch because "that way they

6 A soft-handled pliers is used to prevent the piston from moving as the cylinders are pushed down over the rings (which must be compressed with a ring compressor). You could also accomplish the same thing with a slotted piece of wood.

8 With the heads torqued to factory specifications, the rocker box base is set in place (with new gaskets) and screwed loosely to the rear head. The rocker box base bolts will be tightened to factory torque specs after the rocker arms and shafts are installed.

7 Once the powder-coated cylinders are set in place with new base gaskets between the cylinder and the cases, the heads can be installed. Here the new gasket and O-rings are positioned before the front head is set down.

9 The lifter blocks are installed with new O-rings and a light coating of oil on both the lifter and the lifter block.

11 The pushrods come in two lengths, marked by stripes; three stripes are exhaust while one stripe marks the intake pushrods.

can't slip out of place as you lower the cylinder."

Once the rings are all in the cylinder, the soft-handled pliers is pulled out of the way and the cylinder is pushed down the rest of the way. (Note: A quality boring job includes leaving a chamfered edge at the lower lip of the cylinder to facilitate installation of the cylinders over the rings.) Bug goes through the same procedure for the other cylinder and then sets the head gasket and O-rings in place before installing each head.

Before screwing down the head bolts, he inspects each one to ensure there is no corrosion on the inside or outside and puts a little light oil on the inside threads so he is sure to get a true torque reading. The head bolts are torqued down according to the sequence outlined in the factory service manual. With the heads installed it's time to install the base for the rocker boxes, with new gaskets held in place, again by a little Gasgacinch.

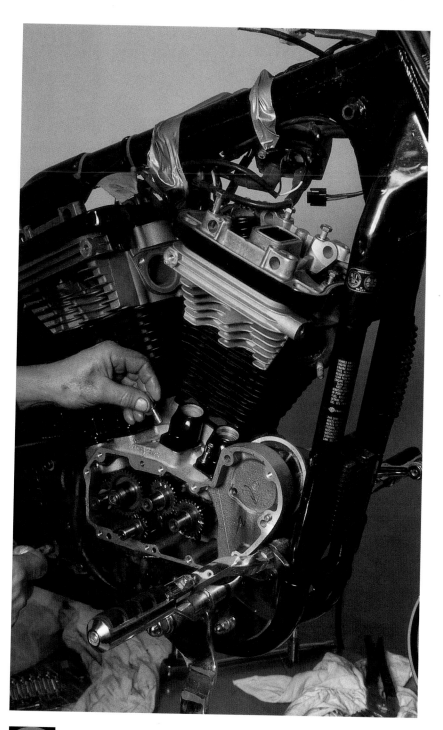

10 All the lifter blocks are installed before the pushrod tubes can be set in place followed by the pushrods themselves.

12 For each cylinder the pushrods must be set in place, the engine turned over so the lifters are at the lowest point in their travel, and then the rocker arms and shafts can be installed.

13 Before snapping the pushrod tubes into place, Bug likes to let the lifters bleed down and then make sure he can turn the pushrods by hand. This ensures that the rocker arms and pushrods are correctly installed.

The lifter blocks, which had been sent out for powder coating, are installed next. Bug installs new sealing O-rings on the lifter blocks, puts an oiled lifter in each one (each lifter and block should be marked so they go back where they came out) puts a little oil on the outside of lifter block itself, and then installs the lifter blocks onto the engine case. Before installing pushrods and tubes, Bug points out the fact that the pushrods come in two lengths, marked by stripes: three stripes signify an exhaust pushrod, while one stripe marks the intake pushrods.

Note: On Sherwood's Sportster, the stock heads and cams were used, but if the heads were shaved or high-performance cams were installed, adjustable pushrods would have had to be used.

Now it's time to install the pushrods and rocker boxes. First, the pushrod tubes are cleaned, new O-rings are installed, and the tubes are collapsed. Bug makes sure to use the right pushrod tube on the right valve, as there are two lengths.

Next, the tubes are set into the lifter blocks, and then the pushrods are set in place from the top. Starting with the rear cylinder, Bug rotates the engine so the lifters are at their lowest point, then installs the rocker arms and shafts, and then finishes tightening the rocker box base bolts.

Before finishing the installation of the pushrod tubes, Bug makes sure the lifters bleed down so he can turn the pushrod by hand. Once he can turn the pushrods by hand, it's time to extend the pushrod tubes into the bottom of the head and then snap the clip in place. He warns against using a screwdriver to fully extend the pushrod tubes if the tubes are plated aluminum because the screwdriver is likely to flake off a big chunk of chrome. Bug adds the comment that Sportsters built after 1991 use one-piece pushrod tubes, which require a different assembly procedure.

After both rocker boxes are tightened down, Bug installs the intake manifold with new O-rings. The intake bolts are positioned so you can't use a torque wrench, and Bug explains, "I just snug the bolts down, because all you're really doing is running the flange down against the head."

He uses a new O-ring gasket on the end of the manifold, lubricated with a little WD-40, and then slides the carburetor in place. Before installing the carb, Bug pulls off the float bowl and installs a slightly larger slow-speed jet.

Now, it's just a matter of reinstalling the coil, the front engine mount, and the various brackets and wires. Bug will set the timing when the engine is first fired, check for leaks, and then the new 1200-cc Sportster is ready to hit the highway.

14 The finished product, a 1200-cc Sportster with powder-coated cylinders and engine covers. An inexpensive hot rod that might surprise a few Big Twins, even with the stock Sportster heads.

CHAPTER 7   *AFTERMARKET V-TWINS*

Contents

Engine Cases 87

Flywheels 91

Cylinders 91

Pistons 92

Heads 92

The Best Combination 95

(Note: Part of this discussion is taken from the *Ultimate V-twin Engine* book, published by Wolfgang Publications and distributed by Motorbooks International.)

If a mild 80-cubic-inch Harley-Davidson engine just won't cut if for your new ride, consider the alternative—an engine built from aftermarket cases, cylinders, heads, and internals. Beware, however, that the number of possible parts and combinations available today is rather overwhelming. This section is intended as an overview of the many options available to the individual building a V-twin from all, or mostly, aftermarket parts.

Before ordering parts you've got to decide exactly how many cubic inches, this motor will be, and how those cubes will be obtained. "Stock" 80-cubic-inch engines have a stroke of 4-1/4 inches and a bore of 3-1/2 inches. They say you can't beat cubic inches, but they don't tell you the best way to get those extra cubic inches.

You can have a 96-cubic-inch engine with a stroker, 4-5/8-inch flywheel mated to a 3-5/8-inch bore. Or you can have a 97-cubic-inch engine with a stock, 4-1/4-inch stroke and a 3-13/16-inch bore. They aren't the same, which isn't to say one is bad and the other is good. They're both good, just different, with different prices, different power delivery, and potentially different longevity.

There is a new emphasis on big-bore cylinders as a means of gaining cubic inches. Proponents of this school often cite the fact that a shorter stroke engine tends to have better reliability—at least in the sense that piston speeds are lower at a given rpm, so ring and piston life are often improved. Short-stroke engines are commonly thought of as being quicker to rev than a similar engine with a smaller bore and longer stroke.

Before beginning work on an engine, most professional engine builders tell their customers to consider what kind of riding they really do, and where in the rpm range they want the power. Use those answers to help determine the number of cubic inches the engine should be and which configuration of bore and stroke best fit your unique situation. You need to decide how big and how powerful an engine you intend to build and kind of work backward from there. Remember, too, that if you stay with conventional dimensions and parts, you save yourself time, trouble, and money.

For example, nearly all cases, cylinders, and heads, up to a bore size of 3-13/16 inches, will use the same cylinder-stud bolt pattern. Most of these parts are compatible with most others. As you move up to bore sizes of 4 inches and more, however, a number of different bolt patterns are used. Most shops still use through-bolts in the larger bore sizes while others bolt the cylinders to the case and the heads to the cylinders.

If you want an engine with a larger bore size, it will not only cost more, but you will also have to be sure the cases, cylinders, and heads are all designed to work together. Many of these big-bore brutes have the lifter bores offset farther to the right to make room for the larger cylinders. This adds one more variable because now the pinion shaft needs to be longer than stock (longer pinion shafts are commonly available).

None of this is intended to discourage you from building, or having built, a motor that's significantly larger than all the other V-twins out there. It is intended to make you think about what you really want—and to make you understand *all* the costs and trade-offs involved in designing and building an engine.

Engine Cases

The engine cases you use for your personal ultimate V-twin will form the foundation for the rest of the engine. They not only support the flywheels, but are the attachment point for the cylinder studs and ultimately the heads.

There are no new Harley-Davidson cases available (unless you have an old set to turn in) so nearly any cases you start out with will come from the aftermarket. Most of the aftermarket cases have addressed and corrected weak areas in some factory cases.

Most cases are made from cast aluminum, which is then machined on sophisticated CNC equipment. The aluminum is commonly 356 T6, which identifies the alloy and the heat treating. The upper end of the case market is occupied by the beautiful billet aluminum cases, which can often be mated to billet cylinders and heads.

If you intend to build an 80-cubic-inch motor, there are a number of engine cases to choose from. Most standard aftermarket cases will accept a stroke of 4-5/8 inches (some up to 5 inches) and a cylinder with a bore up to 3-13/16 inches.

An aftermarket marvel assembled at Minneapolis Custom Cycle: 140 cubic inches of pushrod V-twin built from Merch cases, Hyperformance ductile-iron cylinders, and Walters competition heads. This engine is designed to run in the HDRA Pro Stock class.

Unless you're an experienced V-twin mechanic, you should probably have a shop or trained mechanic assemble the bottom end. In which case, they will likely recommend the brand of cases they prefer.

When you buy the cases, be sure they're well matched to your intended use. If you want big jugs, inquire of the case manufacturer regarding the maximum bore size the cases will accept and any special-order considerations.

Some case manufacturers will bore the cases for cylinder spigots bigger than the cases were originally designed for, before they leave the plant. S&S, Merch Performance Incorporated, and some others offer a matching set of big-bore cylinders in kit form designed to work with their cases.

Many manufacturers have big-bore cases available that will accept

Cast cases, like these from Delkron, can be polished for extra shine. These cases are bored to accept cylinders with a 3-13/16-inch bore.

bores of 4 inches and more. As mentioned, these cases usually use a different stud pattern, which affects your choice of heads as well. Cases designed for a bore of 4 inches and more often have the lifter bores offset to the right (to make room for the big cylinders), which means you must use a longer pinion shaft.

(Note: 1984 and up, Evo-style cases are typically divided into one of two different versions. The 1984-1991 model takes a different oil pump and vents the crankcases differently than do the 1992-and-later cases. S&S notes that there are more subtle differences as well, so the builder should be sure to match the date of the cases to the oil pump.

Most of the cases out there are "good" cases. People do complain, however, that a few brands require extra work to make them truly usable. This extra work might be as simple as cleaning up some threads or as complex as machining the deck surface so it is level on both sides.

Ask around at the various shops and with the manufacturers

Standard Delkron cases will accept a bore size up to 3-7/8 inches and a stroke up to 5 inches. Delkron also manufactures cast cases that accept a bore of up to 4-1/4 inches and billet aluminum four-cam cases that take a bore as large as 4-1/2 inches.

Merch Performance makes street and competition cases, for standard and oversize bores. Pictured are Merch street cases intended for 4-1/4-inch cylinders, which will be combined with a 4-1/4-inch flywheel assembly to make a "square" 120-cubic-inch V-twin.

Long known as proponents of stroker V-twins, S&S now offers the 4-inch-bore long-block assembly. Based on the new special application cases with offset lifter bores, these engines come with a 4-inch bore matched to one of three possible strokes: 4, 4-1/4 or 4-1/2 inches, for total displacements of 100, 107, or 113 cubic inches. *S&S*

to find out which set of cases will provide the strength, internal dimensions, frame-fit, and price that you are looking for.

The cases you buy need to be part of the overall design for the motor. They must work with the cylinders, which must in turn be matched to the heads and pistons. Each part needs to fit all the other parts, your budget, and your intended use.

Engine-Case Buyer's Guide
Delkron Cases

Delkron makes a number of different cases, everything from cast, late-model Evo-style cases to billet four-cam exotica. Most riders and builders will be interested in the cast, Evo-style cases, which accept a bore size up to 3-13/16 inches. Delkron explains that its cases are cast from 356 aluminum, with permanent molds, as opposed to the more common sand-cast

When assembling a complete engine from aftermarket parts, everything must be matched. Some cases use raised decks to make the case stronger, which in turn affects the height of the cylinders. The material the cylinders and pistons are made from will affect their growth rates and ultimately the way they should be fit. Inexperienced builders need to work from "kits" or get recommendations from experienced builders.

At Minneapolis Custom Cycle, where they build everything from "hot rod 80s" to exotic 140-cubic-inch race engines, the flywheel assembly of choice for most 80-inch engines is the stock flywheel from Harley-Davidson (shown). As engine-man Greg Klopp explains, "The quality and price are both really good; you can't beat those parts."

molds. According to Delkron, this means the aluminum is poured at a lower temperature, which results in a more dense molecular matrix and a stronger end product. Delkron is the only case manufacturer to offer a bolt-on sump plate at the bottom of the motor.

If you're the kind of rider who needs maximum cubic inches, Delkron makes another set of cast Evo-style cases with offset lifter bores capable of using a 4-1/4-inch bore. And if you need still more, there's the four-cam billet cases with raised deck and a maximum bore size of 4-1/2 inches.

Merch Performance

A Canadian company, Merch, has long manufactured a variety of cast aluminum V-twin components. Only in the last few years, however, have its parts been readily available in the lower-48 through companies like Mid-USA and a few others. The

Transmission cases for Big Twins come in a variety of styles, including Softail (shown), Dyna, FXR, and FL. The style of case must be matched to your frame. Transmission *cases* are available both from H-D and some aftermarket manufacturers—and can then be filled with gear sets from either H-D or the aftermarket. Complete current production transmissions are available from Harley-Davidson.

These aluminum cylinders with iron liners and aluminum pistons are from S&S, designed to fit its new 4-inch-bore engine. Pistons and cylinders often come as a kit, sometimes with the cylinders already final-honed. If the pistons don't come with the cylinders, your piston choice will be affected by the material the cylinders are made of, the desired static compression ratio, and the design of the combustion chamber.

Merch cases are cast from 356 aluminum heat-treated to a T6 specification. Standard cases will accept a bore up to 3-13/16 inches, though 4- and 4-1/4-inch bores can be accommodated as well. The 4-1/4-inch-bore cases are designed with offset lifter bores to make room for the larger cylinders. As a result, these cases take a longer pinion shaft. Cases can be ordered bare (with right race installed), or as a short or long block mated to Merch cylinders in various dimensions.

STD

STD Development Company has been making cases for V-twins since 1975, and in all that time manager Doug Linscott has seen only two broken cases. "Our cases are sand cast," explains Doug. "Some people say billet is stronger, but ours test to 46,000 psi tensile strength. We feel they're the strongest cases in the industry. The strength comes from the first-run 356 aluminum, and the heat treating that happens after the parts are cast."

Though you can buy a "standard" STD case, Doug explained that STD is a custom manufacturer: "People call me up and tell me how big they think they want the motor and we kind of go from there. We can tailor the cases to a specific project,

including bore sizes all the way up to 4 inches with a half-inch raised deck." STD cases will accept a variety of cylinders, including large-bore cylinders from either Axtell or Hyperformance (addresses for both these companies can be found in the Sources).

STD cases are designed to fit a stock factory frame without modification—and without being a clone of the factory cases. The company recommends flywheel assemblies from S&S for most applications, and occasionally Truett & Osborne Company. Because STD is essentially a custom manufacturer, people there are happy to discuss your project before you get started. "Unless you already have everything figured out, give us a call so we can talk over what's best for your application," explains Doug.

S&S Cycle

Perhaps the best known of all the aftermarket engine-component manufacturers, S&S offers its "Super Stock" cases for sale in permanent-mold 356 aluminum, heat-treated to a T6 specification. Standard cases accept either the stock factory cylinders or the 3-5/8-inch S&S big-bore cylinders. S&S also offers special application crankcases that use offset lifter bores and a longer pinion shaft to accommodate a 4-inch bore—part of its Super Sidewinder package. In addition, the company has new generator cases and even Sportster cases that accept a bore up to 4-3/8 inches, ready for delivery.

S&S cases fit all stock frames (and are also available to fit early Shovel-type frames) and typically ship with the Timken bearings, studs, and the oil pressure sender. Standard cases can accept a stroke all the way to 5 inches and are clearanced for the heavy-duty S&S rods. These cases also feature an oil drain in the bottom of the cases for complete oil changes.

Sputhe Engineering

Sputhe Engineering makes cast Nitralloy cases in a number of variations, from stock replacement cases to big-bore and/or raised-deck examples designed for maximum displacement. Sputhe cases will accept a bore of up to 4 inches, though a bore of 3.78 inches (the size of Sputhe big-bore cylinders) is often combined with a stroke of 4.25 inches to create the Sputhe 95-cubic-inch V-twin.

Flywheels

The flywheel assembly you choose for that new V-twin will likely come from one of three sources: Harley-Davidson, S&S, or Truett & Osborne. If your engine comes as a partial kit, then the flywheel assembly will come with the cases and other parts, and may even be installed. Most case manufacturers will recommend a particular flywheel assembly.

Flywheel Buyer's Guide
S&S

The S&S catalog lists a rather large variety of flywheel assemblies, including wheels of two diameters, 8-1/2 or 8-1/4 inches. While most stock V-twins run a flywheel of 8-1/2 inches, the smaller wheels are useful for stroker engines. Stroker engines bring the piston much closer to the flywheels at the bottom of each stroke. Because of this, it is often necessary to use a piston with a short skirt area, which in turn makes for a piston that wobbles in the cylinder. The smaller diameter flywheels (which S&S recommends for 98- and 103-inch SideWinders) means you can build that stroker motor and still use a more stable piston with a longer skirt.

Truett & Osborn

Truett & Osborn in Wichita, Kansas, offers flywheels from 4-1/4 inches all the way up to a full 5-1/4 inches. These flywheels are made from ductile iron and heat-treated before being machined. Complete flywheel assemblies are offered as well, including special-order items with longer pinion shafts.

Harley-Davidson

Harley-Davidson offers its stock, 4-1/4-inch flywheel assemblies for sale from any dealership. George Edwards, of St. Paul Harley-Davidson, feels these are very high-quality parts: "The factory has invested in plenty of new tooling in the last few years," he says. "The flywheels, for example, are a three-piece assembly where the aftermarket assemblies are five pieces, with separate pinion and sprocket shafts that bolt into the flywheel on either side."

Cylinders

For street use, cylinders break down into two basic materials: aluminum with a liner made from cast iron, or solid cast iron (in a few instances ductile iron is used on the street). As always, each material has advantages and disadvantages, and everyone seems to have an opinion.

Advocates of cast iron cite the fact that cast iron doesn't "grow" with heat as fast as aluminum, so the compression ratio cold is the same as it is hot. Cast-iron cylinders are said to be more stable and distort less as well, meaning a better ring seal and improved oil control. The downside to all this cast-iron business is its inability to give up heat to the surrounding air. How big a problem that is depends on whom you talk to.

Designers in the aluminum camp like the non-ferrous material for its light weight and willingness to conduct heat to the air, which they feel results in lower combustion chamber and oil-film temperatures, and prolonged engine life.

Dan Haak, an engineer at S&S, explains that they take the growth of aluminum into account when they design the parts, so it presents less of a problem than people might think. He feels that because the expansion rate of the cylinder and piston are nearly the same, the piston fit cold can be tighter than it might be with a cast-iron cylinder and aluminum piston. This means less noise and an improved seal, cold or hot. He also feels that the lower cylinder temperatures seen with aluminum cylinders have a significant impact on reducing the tendency to detonation and piston scuffing.

Cylinder Buyer's Guide
Axtell

Axtell cylinders come in two materials, cast-iron or ductile iron. Most of the cast-iron cylinders go out the door in sizes up to 3-13/16 inches, though Axtell can bore the cast iron up to maximum of 4 inches. This requires a different bolt pattern than stock. Ductile iron cylinders intended for competition use can be bored all the way to 4-1/2 inches. Cylinders from Axtell can be shipped with or without pistons, which are available in a wide variety of styles.

Harley-Davidson

If the engine you're building is an 80-cubic-inch mill, consider stock H-D cylinders and matching pistons. The cylinders are cast aluminum with cast-iron sleeves, and commonly go well past 50,000 miles without any trouble.

Hyperformance

Hyperformance manufactures ductile iron cylinders with fins that will accept a bore size up to 5.1 inches. In addition, it handles billet and cast aluminum cylinders from other manufacturers, which are also intended for larger-than-average bore sizes.

Merch

A variety of big-bore cylinders in cast aluminum with cast-iron liners are available from Merch. Bore sizes start at 3-13/16 inches, and go all the way to 4-1/4 inches for a square 120-cubic-inch V-twin. Cylinders can be ordered bare or with matching JE forged pistons.

Sputhe

Sputhe Engineering has manufactured cast aluminum cylinders with cast-in sleeves since 1977. Cylinders are cast in 383 aluminum alloy. The aluminum is injected into a steel die at over 5,000 psi, assuring a perfect bond to the lascomite sleeve. Lascomite is a high-tensile chrome-moly alloy, tougher and less brittle than cast iron. The 3.78-inch Nitralloy cylinders are cast with additional fin area in a symmetrical pattern to reduce thermal distortion. These cylinders are stock height, so studs, pushrods, and exhaust pipes of stock dimension can be used. Matching "zero clearance" forged pistons with cam and barrel-shaped skirt configurations are available.

S&S Cycle

S&S cylinders, made from cast aluminum with cast-iron liners, are available with or without matching pistons. These cylinders come in various lengths to work with strokes from 4-1/4 to 5 inches. Stroke must be considered when ordering pistons as well, so there is adequate clearance at the bottom of the piston for flywheels and the other piston. S&S also has a 4-inch-bore aluminum cylinder meant for street use.

Pistons

Pistons come in various shapes, manufactured from either cast or forged aluminum. Forged aluminum is typically stronger than cast aluminum, thus we all think we need forged pistons. The forged-or-cast controversy is another instance in which things aren't as simple as they seem.

Up until a few years ago forged pistons had to be fit somewhat loosely, in anticipation of the fact that the pistons would expand as they warmed up. Cast pistons on the other hand were made from a different aluminum alloy, one with a high silicone content to slow down the growth rate. Thus the cast pistons could be fit more tightly than forged.

The new crop of forged pistons contain silicone, however. Thus the growth rate for these new forged slugs is nearly the same as with cast pistons. Some builders and manufacturers, however, still

The Harley heads feature the classic D-shaped combustion chamber, normally matched to a flat-top piston. Standard valve sizes are 1.85 inches and 1.615 inches for intake and exhaust. Heads and pistons must be carefully chosen to achieve the right compression ratio and so the combustion chamber and piston dome shapes are complementary.

prefer a cast piston. In the end, most of us will have to rely on the engine builder or cylinder/head manufacturer for a recommendation as to the best piston to run.

Heads

There are plenty of heads out there, from used factory castings to billet four-valve designs. At least one well known builder, Dan Fitzmaurice from Zipper's, suggests that you choose the heads first, not last, and then make sure everything else (pistons, cylinders, and all the rest) are compatible with the heads.

Your new heads have to match the stud pattern for the engine. As mentioned earlier, most bore sizes up to 3-13/16 inches use a standardized stud pattern. Bore sizes of 4 inches and larger, however, use one of a number of stud patterns.

The heads must be matched to the pistons. Some heads work fine with a flat-top piston while others need a domed piston that fits finger-and-glove into the recess of the cylinder head. Be sure to ask the head manufacturer for a recommendation with regard to the pistons you use—which will best complement the combustion-chamber shape and which combination will provide the compression ratio you've decided upon.

If you are relying heavily on your local V-twin engine builder for advice, you might want to take that advice when it comes to choosing the heads. If you're assembling a "known combination" of parts, then it doesn't make much sense to deviate from that plan.

Consider that among all the new companies bringing heads to the market, not all will be here in three or five years. Try to buy from a company with a good reputation, one that puts good-quality components in its heads And a company that will be there the next time you pull the engine apart for a rebuild or further improvements.

If you want heads with really big flow numbers, it is sometimes cheaper in the long run to buy a more expensive set of heads than it is to buy cheap and then pay a high per-hour figure to have extensive porting done. And while we all want heads with good flow numbers, there is such a thing as too big a port on a head meant for street use. A final note on flow: Be sure to ask the manufacturer for its flow charts before paying for the new, trick cylinder heads.

While dual-plugging the heads for your new Evo-style V-twin adds to the sex appeal and in some cases the horsepower, it isn't necessary on most hot street engines. In fact, some head manufacturers recommend against the installation of the second spark plug.

Cylinder-Head Buyer's Guide
Edelbrock

Long known for its automotive parts, Edelbrock has entered the V-twin market with a pair of cast heads intended to offer increased performance for V-twins.

RevTech heads are cast from 356 aluminum and come in standard and high-compression versions. These heads feature raised intake ports for better flow, yet still use stock intake manifolds. Big-bore versions are available for Big Twin engines, as are complete Sportster heads.

The first head the company introduced, the Performer, comes with a 1.850-inch intake and 1.610-inch exhaust valves, a D-shaped exhaust port (which accepts all stock-style exhaust systems), and a rectangular-shaped intake port.

More recently, Edelbrock has introduced a second head known as the Performer RPM head. This second model comes with larger, 1.94-inch and 1.625-inch valves, and "CNC ported" passages. The Performer RPM is available in two combustion chamber sizes and comes with high-test springs and titanium retainers, designed to allow the use of camshafts with a lift up to 0.650 inch. If you would rather do the finish work on the valves yourself, the Performer RPM heads are available in a "raw" configuration.

Feuling Four-Valve

It was only a matter of time before four-valve heads, now used on many high-performance automobiles (and some Grand Prix cars and bikes early in this century), would "cross over" to the land of V-twins. In essence, two small

holes can be made to pass more air than one big one. By using two smaller ports, total flow can often be increased (especially at modest valve lifts) while still maintaining good velocity through the ports.

Feuling cast heads come in various stages, starting with a kit that uses the stock carburetor and Feuling anti-reversion exhaust pipes with the four-valve heads. Stage II kits include a dual-carb intake, so you can hang one carburetor on either side of the bike, and a compatible high-performance camshaft. For the truly serious horsepower junkies, Feuling offers stages III through V.

Johnson Performance Engineering

One of the "new kids on the block," Alan Johnson usually spends his time manufacturing billet heads for Top Fuel cars. That same expertise has now been used to manufacture a complete V-twin head that is shaped by CNC machines from a raw chunk of 6061 T6 aluminum.

These new heads come with their own intake manifold and accept stock and aftermarket two-bolt exhaust systems. Designed for

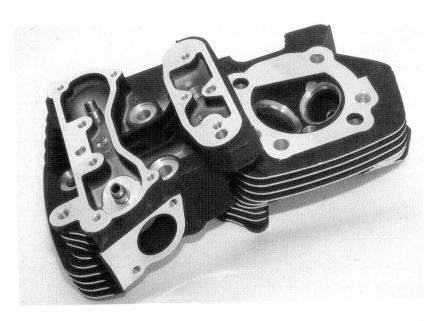

These cast heads from Harley-Davidson can be ordered either assembled or bare, already painted, and sized to fit standard cylinder stud patterns.

single-spark-plug use, these heads are available from Johnson Engineering.

Merch Performance Inc.

From Canada comes a cast head with CNC-machined, bathtub-shaped combustion chambers. A raised intake port helps to increase flow, all the way to 150 cfm at 10 inches of water with the 1.900-inch intake valves at 0.500-inch lift (without any additional porting work). Merch heads can be ordered with bigger valves, four-bolt exhaust, and early- or late-style breathing. You can even order Merch heads to fit bores of 4 inches and more.

Patrick Racing

Billet aluminum heads from Nigel Patrick come in various stages of "high performance." The basic head features a 76-cc combustion chamber and 1.94- and 1.60-inch intake and exhaust valves. Options include non-stock valve angles and some very large diameter valves—all the way to 2.25 inches for intakes and 2.00 inches for exhausts. Though Patrick makes heads for your stock

Evo, the polished billet heads are more commonly seen atop a large-bore motor like a Keck.

RevTech

One of the first large aftermarket companies to offer a complete, ready-to-install cylinder head, RevTech now offers its heads in both stock and big-bore configurations; in stock- and high-compression models.

These aluminum heads are cast from 356 alloy, heat-treated to T6. The stainless steel valves measure 1.940 and 1.610 inches, respectively, for the intake and exhaust. Though the intake ports have been raised from the factory location, these heads will accept all stock intake manifolds. Three-piece valve springs and heavy-duty retainers allow the use of camshafts with lifts up to 0.600 inch. RevTech heads can also be ordered "raw" to be finished by the engine builder of your choice.

Rivera Engineering

Rivera Engineering offers for sale two versions of its billet four-valve heads, one designed for bore

sizes up to 3-13/16 inches and another for monster motors with bore sizes up to 4-1/4 inches.

Designed as a bolt-on improvement for most Evos, these heads accept stock intake manifolds and exhaust pipes. Access to the centrally located spark plug is said to be much improved when compared to earlier cast four-valve heads offered by Rivera.

S&S

These cast aluminum cylinder heads feature a 2-inch intake and a 1.610-inch exhaust valve. Both the intake and exhaust ports use a unique shape; the intake in particular uses a vertical vane intended to help route the incoming charge around the intake valve.

S&S heads come with their own manifold, one with a horizontal vane meant to create controlled turbulence and aid in complete burning. The exhaust ports use standard mounting dimensions so stock and aftermarket exhaust systems will bolt on without modification. The combustion chamber is a closed, high-quench chamber, which necessitates the use of S&S pistons.

S&S heads do not come taped for dual plugs, and S&S feels that "the superior mixture flow and turbulence also provide excellent flame travel. . . dual spark plug configurations for normal operation are not needed or recommended."

In addition to the standard head, S&S offers a completely new head designed for its 4-inch-bore engines. This new head has the correct stud spacing for the new bore diameters and is designed to work with a flat-top piston.

STD

This cast head with the "bathtub" chamber normally comes in a raw configuration. That way your engine builder (or STD) can install seats and valves matched to the engine size and use, and add any

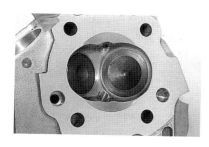

The RevTech head comes with 1.94-inch intake valves and 1.61-inch exhaust valves set in a semi-bathtub combustion chamber. Standard complete heads include three-piece valve springs and high-quality retainers that will accept cams with lifts up to 0.600 inches. The heads you buy must fit the stud pattern of your engine and be matched to the pistons.

porting work they feel is necessary. These high-performance heads feature a raised intake port for improved port shape and a four-bolt pattern on the exhaust port so either a stock- or flanged-style exhaust can be used. Despite the raised intake port, these heads will accept stock intake manifolds. These heads are available in either a single-plug or a dual-plug configuration.

In addition to their raw head castings with the bathtub combustion chamber, STD is currently offering a ready-to-wear cylinder head. This new head will come completely assembled with 1.840-inch intake and 1.610-inch exhaust valves.

Sputhe

Sputhe cast heads come in two variations, the small version designed for 80-inch Evos, or the larger version for 95-cubic-inch and larger engines with bore sizes of 3-13/16 inches. These heads feature a large fin area for better cooling and raised intake ports for improved flow. Buyers can choose between aluminum, bronze or manganese-meehanite valve guides. Intake valves are one-piece stainless forgings, while the exhaust valves are titanium-nitride coated one-piece austenitic forgings. Valve springs can be ordered to best match the acceleration and lift of your camshaft.

Before You Bolt the Heads On

Whether the heads you are bolting to that new V-twin are heavily modified castings from a company like STD, or nearly stock units from The Motor Company, there are a few things to consider before you bolt them on. Your list of possible concerns includes:

1. Possible valve-to-valve clearance problems. To quote Wickstrom from Kokesh MC, "As you get into wilder cams and heads with bigger and bigger valves, you need to pay more attention to this matter."

2. Possible valve-spring coil bind. You need to know the dimension of the spring when it "stacks." With the head assembled (with a light spring) and the valve depressed to "maximum lift," compare the dimension between the spring retainers to the coil-bind figure. Most cam and valve-gear manufacturers recommend that you have 0.050 to 0.060 inch extra clearance between maximum lift and coil bind. It's obvious that you shouldn't lift the valve to the point where the spring hits coil bind. Less obvious is the fact that if your cam-head-spring combination has the spring *near* its coil-bind limit at each camshaft rotation the springs will soon fatigue.

3. With the valves at maximum lift, you also need to ensure that there is at least 0.050 inch of clearance between the top of the valve guide/seal and the bottom of the upper spring retainer.

4. Though you need clearance before coil bind, you also need a spring with enough pressure to keep the lifter rollers following the cam lobes at high rpm. Some builders like to use a set of springs matched to the camshaft, but even then you need to check for coil bind and clearance to the top of the valve guide.

5. Valve-to-piston clearance. Though it sounds like too much extra work, professional builders recommend assembling the engine with clay on the valve pockets of the pistons, rotating the engine by hand a few times, and then disassembling to make sure the clay is at least 0.080 inches thick where the valve came closest to the piston.

The Best Combination

As the aftermarket offerings continue to expand, it's harder and harder to know what to buy. One of the interesting things about the Evolution Big Twin engine design is the almost infinite number of combinations that can be built. Nearly any displacement from 80 to over 150 cubic inches is available. Even if you know how many inches you want, there's still the question of how best to obtain that displacement.

Unless you build engines for a living, it's often best to seek out competent advice from people who do. It's easier to work with a known combination of parts that have been tried before and that have a track record than it is to start from scratch with combinations that haven't been tried. "Engine modeling" with a computer program (like the Accelerator program mentioned earlier in the chapter) can take some of the surprises out of engine building.

In terms of quality, most of the parts are good, including the stuff made in Milwaukee, though some components work better in combination with certain other parts, or are better suited to a particular application. Which brings us back to the fact that the first thing to figure out before building an engine is exactly what you want that engine to do.

CHAPTER 8 SHEET METAL

Contents

The New Stuff 96

Mock-Up 97

Mounting 97

Equipment for a
Basic Shop 101

Tools 101

Welding Sheet Metal 102

Safety 103

Build It from Scratch and
Throw Away the Catalog .104

Materials 104

Sheet Metal
Case Studies 106

When it comes to new sheet metal for your ride there are at least three options: Buy new sheet metal (which may turn out to be fiberglass or plastic), modify the existing sheet metal that came with the bike, or build new designs from scratch. This chapter follows that same outline. You will find a discussion of the various shapes available from the catalogs, a brief look at the most common sheet metal modification projects, and a final section on building from scratch.

The New Stuff

Because of the explosion in the custom motorcycle market, more and more shapes are available. Up until just a few years ago the only available sheet metal was the standard replacement parts and a few "custom" front and rear fenders from Drag Specialties or Custom Chrome.

Arlen Ness was one of the first to offer builders something really different with his Taildragger and Cafe fender designs. Today we have unique fender designs from Rick Doss, Jesse James, and Pro One, to name but a few. These shapes run the gamut from little bikini fenders to full length Street Sweepers as well as paneled designs from Milwaukee Iron.

Harley-Davidson makes available all the standard sheet metal seen on its bikes, including the classic FL front fender in a "smooth" version without any trim or holes-for-trim. One of the more popular front fenders seen lately on bikes with a 16-inch front wheel is the Fat Boy front fender with the flip at the trailing edge. You can even order sheet metal from the local Harley-Davidson store already painted. (See Chapter 9 for more on the Harley-Davidson factory paint program.)

In fact, some riders are ordering a complete, and painted, second set of sheet metal from the dealer. That way they can have a "convertible" and change the look of the bike simply by installing the other set of sheet metal.

Like the new fender designs, gas tanks have shown a similar tendency to evolve into new shapes at a bewildering speed. All the current catalogs offer Fat Bob tanks in 3.5-, 5-, and even 6-gallon sizes. You can still weld "tails" on your Fat Bob tanks, though Drag Specialties and others now offer steel tanks with steel tails already installed. Just add Bondo and sand to suit. More exotic designs are available, too—stretched one-piece tanks formed by hand from aluminum, available from a variety of sources. These new-wave stretched tanks include extra long examples intended to be used on stretched frames, as well as 3-gallon models designed to bolt onto a stock Softail frame.

If you're riding a Sportster, a group of mini Fat Bob types of tanks are sold under various trade names and designed to give the Sportster the look of a Big Twin. You can complete the Big Twin look with a Fat Bob style rear fender, designed again to fit the Sporty frame.

This Fat-Bob-style tank is actually a one piece tank intended to fit FXR chassis and give those bikes the classic twin-tank look. Use nearly any standard Fat Bob dash or speedometer to finish the look. *Custom Chrome*

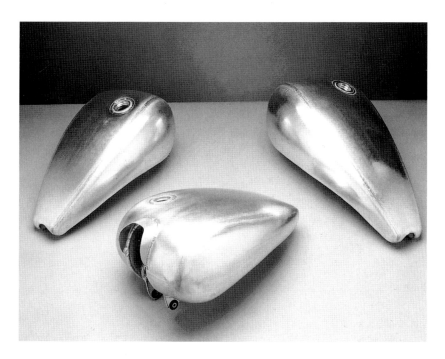

If you're looking for something slimmer, trimmer, and sexier than a Fat Bob, consider a hand-formed aluminum tank. Available in three versions, these tanks fit stock Softail frames and frames with 2 and 5 inches of stretch. *Custom Chrome*

Mock-Up

The fenders and gas tank(s) you choose will have to fit the bike, both in a mechanical sense and also aesthetically. If you're building a serious custom, you probably went to the trouble of sketching up the design for the new machine as described in Chapter 1. When you get the new sheet metal parts, it's an excellent idea to do a complete mock-up with the bike on a hoist before sending everything out for paint.

You need to do the mock-up because the "bolt on" parts sometimes don't, which means you need to be sure all the holes line up. Some aftermarket fenders and tanks don't come with holes at all, in which case you need to clamp the parts to the bike and then figure out where to drill the holes and how to fabricate the brackets.

The mock-up phase also gives you a chance to really examine the bike before you commit to painting all the parts. This exercise works better if the bike is up off the floor and you can stand back far enough to really "see" as it will look out on the street. If the rear fender you just bought doesn't look right, go borrow another one and try that one. Spend time trying each part in slightly different positions, a small change in the location of a tank or fender can have a profound effect on the bike's overall appearance. All the parts need to work together and fit the overall look for the bike.

Mounting

Motorcycles, and Harley-Davidsons in particular, have this nasty habit of vibrating, which makes it doubly important that all the parts be mounted correctly. There's nothing worse than a gas tank that cracks at one of the mounts, or a fender that falls down on the tire as you're going down the highway (not a funny situation).

When it comes to mounting a gas tank on the bike, it's best to follow the immortal words of bike-builder Dave Perewitz: "People try to use all kinds of hidden trick mounts, and they don't support the tank in the right areas. At our shop we try to keep the stock mounting arrangements whenever we can. If we can't, then we try to keep as close to stock as possible."

Stock Fat Bob tanks come in two varieties. Most popular and most common are the 1984 and later examples known as "flat-sided" tanks. These tanks mount to the frame with rubber grommets, as opposed to the earlier Fat Bob Tanks that bolt directly to the frame. If you're mounting a pair of Fat Bob tanks on a bike that came with the wrong mounts or no mounts at all, kits are available from all the major catalog companies to

Some of the highest quality sheet metal available for your bike comes from Harley-Davidson. Tanks are carefully welded, sealed, and guaranteed. You can even buy the sheet metal with paint already applied.

This Quick Bob fiberglass fender is designed to give your Sportster the look of a Big Twin. Available to fit nearly any Sportster from early iron-head versions to current XL models. *Drag Specialties*

adapt either early or late-style Fat Bob tanks to any frame.

Many Harley-Davidsons come from the factory with tanks bolted directly to the frame. If you're working with a solid-mount tank, adapting an FXR tank to a Sportster, for example, be sure the new mounting tabs are welded on by someone who can create a non-brittle weld that doesn't add stress to the tank.

When it comes to mounting fenders, remember that the tire grows in diameter with speed. So while it might look really cool to have the front fender mounted right down there on top of the tire, one millimeter of clearance might turn to zero millimeters at 70 or 80 miles per hour.

The bigger the fender is, the more it needs some extra support. Yet we all want that clean look with a minimum of brackets and bolts. A lip welded all the way around the edge, or a piece of heavy strap welded or fiberglassed into the inside of the fender will help provide the missing support.

Clean fender lines are offered in this Legacy fender, made from fiberglass. Available in two widths, 7-1/2 and 8-1/2 inches. Note the billet fender strut complete with turn signals. *Arlen Ness Inc.*

California fabricator Steve Davis likes to use button-head bolts inside the fender and he makes sure they point up or out. "So even if the tire does touch the bolt it isn't hitting a sharp edge that will tear the tire. People tend to ignore what might happen when the suspension bottoms hard. You need to know how the geometry works—does the tire move though an unusual arc as the suspension compresses? Can the tire hit a bolt head or trailing edge of the fender at the end of its travel? It sounds obvious, but people miss things like that all the time."

Speaking of obvious, it's a good idea to use self-locking nuts or plenty of Loctite when installing the fenders. Self-locking Nylock-type nuts are especially handy when mounting plastic or fiberglass

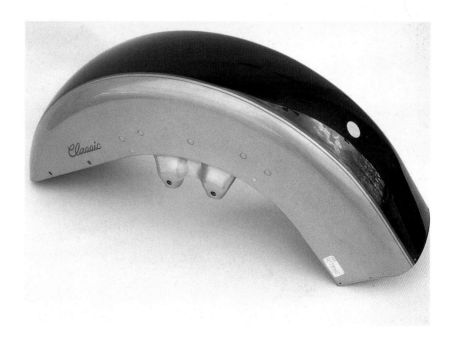

Fat fenders never go out of style, and among the most popular of all the fat fender shapes is this "dresser" front fender from Harley-Davidson. This fender is also available without paint and without any mounting holes.

This Frontdragger fender offers the tail-dragger look in a narrow front fender designed to fit 19- and 21-inch front wheels. Made of fiberglass. *Arlen Ness Inc.*

fenders because they provide a positive lock without the need to super-tighten the nut. To keep the wires that run inside most rear fenders out of the way, some shops weld small diameter tubing way up into the corner of the fender, or secure the wiring harness into the corner of the fender with silicone or fiberglass. If part of your modifications include a fat rear tire be sure it can't hit the tabs on the inside of many factory fenders.

Equipment for a Basic Shop

No matter how big your shop is, the work area must be well lit and have good ventilation. You need compressed air (more later), heat, and plenty of electrical outlets. The shop needs a floor that can be kept clean, and access to running water is a nice bonus.

If you live in a part of the country with cold winters, consider the flammable liquids in the shop before you choose a heat source. Remember that gas and solvent fumes are usually heavier than air, so they fall to the floor. This means that if there are any flames or pilot lights or sparks in

This shot illustrates the small shrinker-stretcher at the Metal Fab shop. Though the tool is set up for stretching (the metal is spread out slightly each time you bring down the handle) a change in the jaws will allow it to shrink as well (it will gather up the metal under the jaws).

the shop you must keep them as high off the floor as possible. And though a 50-gallon converted wood burner may seem like a cheap source of heat, it could turn out to be less than economical if it causes the shop to burn down (it *can* happen to you).

If you're going to do the finish work as well as the actual fabrication, then you need to be able to heat the shop to a nice steady 70 degrees minimum, and keep it there long enough for the various paint and body finishing materials to dry or cure.

Tools

Davis suggests that you really don't need an awful lot of tools to

A factory Fat Boy rear fender makes a nice swoopy shape popular with many customizers.

WELDING SHEET METAL

Fabricating parts from sheet metal often means making up smaller sub-assemblies and then welding those together to make the finished piece. Welding sheet metal is a specialized skill, one that is only acquired after much practice. Before starting in on your first sheet-metal welding job, heed the advice of Jim Petrykowski, owner of Metal Fab in Blaine, Minnesota. Petrykowski offers the following advice for first-time fabricators:

1. Always use welding rod that is better quality than the steel you're welding together so you add strength to the weld. This may mean checking with a welding shop to ensure you're using the right rod or wire. Don't assume that what came with the welder is the best rod for the job.
2. Use a heli-arc welder for sheet metal, if possible.
3. Be sure the parts fit together nicely, so the welding is easier and you're not trying to fill big gaps. If the steel is 1/16-inch thick use 1/16-inch rod or filler.
4. Don't overlay parts; it's not stronger. Always use butt welds.
5. Try to keep the heat low and contained to limit the amount of warpage.
6. Be careful not to overheat the weld when you grind it; if you overheat the weld, you will weaken it.

2 Roehl stops occasionally to view the work and adjust the edge with a small hammer. If he were welding two pieces of sheet, Roehl would probably use a hammer on one side while holding a dolly on the other.

1 This sequence of photos shows the essentials of welding sheet metal. The work is being done by Rob Roehl, fabricator for Donnie Smith. The project involves welding in a panel on a Fat Bob tank so the tank wraps nearly around the frame's top tube just behind the neck. After cutting and tack-welding the piece in place, the welds are done as a series of stitches, so as to avoid heat build-up. The welding is done with the heli-arc or TIG welder. The material is 14-gauge, cold-rolled steel. Note how well the piece fits the tank, so there are no gaps to fill.

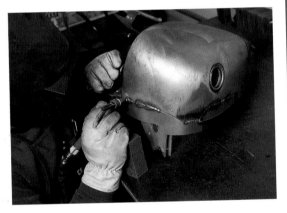

3 Moving across the piece prevents the concentration of too much heat in one spot. Roehl takes the occasional break between stitches to let everything cool. Almost finished, note the neat, even welded seam and the lack of warpage. The sheet metal panels are 14 gauge, which seems heavy, but Roehl explains, "The 14 gauge works well because the piece just stands there, so it needs some strength, and the curve on the front piece is pretty gentle so it's not hard to shape. You could make these pieces from lighter material, but you might have to provide some support from behind."

To make a custom seat, you first need a seat-pan. You can see that this seat-pan at Donnie Smith's shop is essentially made of two pieces. The most interesting is the rear piece, which was shrunk along the edges so it would follow the contours of the fender.

get started. A couple of body hammers with matching dollies, some tin snips, a bag of shot, and maybe some type of soft-faced hammer. An assortment of "garage junk" is always handy as an aid in shaping and forming the panels. Pipes in various sizes can be a great aid in forming simple curves, and a piece of angle iron can be used as a "brake" when clamped to the bench.

You will also need a ruler and possibly a square, along with a good scribe and possibly a can of bluing to make it easier to see the scribed line. Because a conventional fluted drill bit leaves an oblong hole when you drill through sheet metal, a stepped drill is a good idea for drilling holes in sheet metal. A set of countersink bits will allow you to de-burr the hole after you drill it, or help to get that screw head flush with the surface of the sheet metal.

Beyond that it's a matter of your budget, how involved you intend to get, and how much finish work you want to do. Small brakes for making neat bends in sheet metal are available for the small shop, as are small shrinker-stretchers. Experienced (and well-funded) builders may have somewhat exotic tools like an English wheel for putting a soft crown in a piece of metal.

If you're going to do your own finish work, you need a grinder and/or a double-action (DA) sander for sanding the plastic filler. Remember that when it comes to grinders, it's better to use a small grinder that affects only the area you need to finish. Large grinders tend to gouge the metal and add a tremendous amount of heat. How much finish work you do will also affect the size of the compressor you buy. In the real world you should probably have at least a 3-horsepower compressor, though 5

won't be too large if you're going to use plenty of air tools and do your own spray painting. (See Chapter 8 for more on air compressors.)

Getting started on some sheet metal projects is easier than doing your first engine overhaul. The tools you need to begin with don't cost as much as one Snap-On ratchet, and the fixtures can be bought for the price of scrap at the local metals yard. What this requires isn't tools or technique but rather the willingness to go out in the shop and simply give it a try

Safety

You will come into contact with a variety of potentially toxic materials and dangerous situations in nearly any small fabrication shop. The dangers include air-borne dust, toxic liquids and vapors, paint, flying debris, and noise.

To protect yourself from sanding and grinding dust, always wear at least a good dust filter and eye protection during any work in the shop. The goggles will protect your eyes from flying debris from the grinder and also prevent vapors from being absorbed by the mucous membranes around your eyes. Air-powered grinders and cut-off wheels do their work fast and make a tremendous amount of noise as they do. Buy a set of "ear muffs" and hang them where you can reach them before you pull the trigger on the air tool or electric grinder. For spray painting, follow the safety guidelines in Chapter 9.

Sheet metal is very prone to super-sharp edges, so a pair of good leather work gloves is a good idea and also makes it easier to get a good grip on the metal as you work.

Make it a habit as you work through each day to use dust filters, eye and ear protection, and respirators for painting. Do it even when you're really in a hurry. You'll be happy years from now that you did.

Build It from Scratch and Throw Away the Catalog

There's only one way I know of to have truly unique parts, and that's to build them yourself (or have them built). Sometimes, after you've cut, spliced, and extended a fender or air dam, you might wonder if it wouldn't have been easier to just build it from scratch.

By starting with an existing fender or gas tank you make the job both easier and more difficult. Easier because you have much of the basic shape before you even start—harder because if you want a radical design the existing shape will be more of a hindrance than a help.

In some cases you are forced to make the part from a sheet of steel or aluminum simply because what you want doesn't exist.

Changing the radius of this fender so it would fit a 16-inch tire was done by carefully cutting a series of slits along the edge on both sides. What they've actually done is shrink the sides before the new skirting was added. If you don't have access to shrinking equipment this is one way to do it, though there is a considerable amount of labor involved.

Remember, each piece will have to fit the next perfectly and you (or someone you hire) will have to do a very nice job of welding all the pieces into a whole.

Materials

So you've got a sketch, you've even gone so far as to create the new part from light board. It's time to start cutting, but you still aren't sure whether it should be made from steel or aluminum.

As always, there are two sides to every argument and every material choice. Steel is easier to buy, weld, and paint. Aluminum, on the other hand, is softer so it shapes more easily, but it's harder for most of us to paint or weld.

If the part doesn't require a great deal of shaping, steel is probably the logical choice. Special "drawing-quality" or "aluminum-killed" sheet steel is easier to shape. This sheet steel is formed by adding a little bit of aluminum at the end of the steel-making process. The aluminum gives the steel its name and a more malleable nature. Finding this easy-to-work sheet steel can be hard unless there's a big stamping facility nearby where you can buy their scrap. If you can't find drawing-quality steel at least buy cold-rolled, not hot-rolled, sheet.

Light sheet is easy to form, but it has limited strength and burns easily when welded. Twenty gauge

Here you can see how Rob Roehl moved the upper mount on these late-model Fat Bob tanks so he could run a trim dash that follows the contour of the tanks.

is the lightest sheet steel most shops use for any fabricating projects, and 18 is more common. Sixteen gauge is nice and strong; it's almost twice as thick as 20 gauge and at least twice as tough to shape. In the real world, 20 gauge is what current automotive sheet metal is made from, while 16 is the gauge they stamped fenders and door skins from in the good old 1950s.

Though decimals aren't often used to describe steel, 20 gauge measures 0.035 inch, 18 is equal to 0.045 inch, and a micrometer clamped onto a piece of 16-gauge steel will show a reading of 0.063 inch.

Aluminum *is* measured in decimals; common sheet dimensions include 0.050 and 0.060 inch. The exact alloy of aluminum will determine its properties; the 6061 billet material we hear so much about is a poor choice for a shaping project. Much better are the more "pure" aluminum alloys like the 1100 series or perhaps the 3000 series (3003 is a common sheet alloy used for fabrication projects). Though you might want your new billet wheel material hardened to a T-6 specification, a non-heat-treated sheet is much easier to shape and work.

As Davis is fond of saying: "Every shape you make involves either shrinking or stretching." When you're making parts for your Harley-Davidson, remember that it's easier to stretch the material than it is to shrink it. This is especially true in the home or small shop.

FABRICATION OF A SIMPLE DASH IN DONNIE SMITH'S SHOP

Like all good sheet metal projects, this one starts with a sketch and then a template laid out on light board. Though some of the dashes that Rob Roehl, fabricator for Donnie Smith, makes consist of a long piece that actually stands up off the tanks, this one is going to be more of a pancake design. "Because it doesn't have tall sides," explains Roehl, "I'm just going to hammer it out of one piece without making sides."

Once the template is created and Roehl is sure it fits bike, the dimensions are transferred to the sheet steel. While he is marking the outline of the part on the sheet metal, Roehl also lays out a centerline, which makes a nice reference all through the project.

After cutting the piece out on a band saw Roehl begins bending the edges over a piece of pipe. "The key is patience," explains Roehl. "People

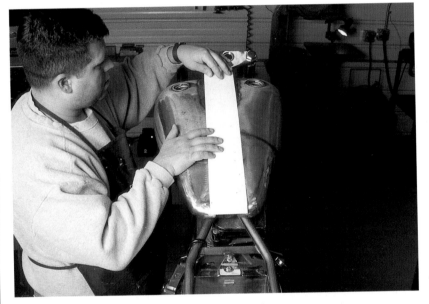

1 Good designs—even simple ones—start with a sketch followed by a template made from light board. Here Rob Roehl test fits the template on the actual tanks.

2 Once he's happy with the shape of the template, Roehl transfers those dimensions to the sheet steel. One of the dimensions he transfers is the centerline of the piece, which makes a good reference throughout the project. Though he uses a saw, this material could be cut with a sheers and a tin snips. You need to cut sheet metal with tools that won't damage or distort the edge.

shouldn't try to do it too fast. As you bend the steel at the edges they stretch and then the piece picks up a curve, which isn't what you want but you can work it out by hand. For the actual hammering I like to use a plastic hammer because it doesn't dent the metal itself."

As the piece starts to take on the right shape, Roehl changes to a new fixture with a smaller tube to make tighter bends (most of these "fixtures" were made in the shop). Once the edges are rolled, Roehl starts to bend the dash the long way so it will follow the contour of the tanks. He rolls it carefully by hand, with many trial fits in-between. "I like to do as much as I can by hand before using the ham-

mer, because it's so easy to go too far with the hammer," he says.

Next he rolls the upper edge around the edge of the tanks. "I don't know if I should shrink the edge or not to get the end to curl more," he explains.

After more hammer work on the round end, Roehl does another trial fit.

3 Roehl rolls the edge over a homemade fixture using a plastic hammer, explaining, "I like the plastic hammer because it doesn't dent the metal itself."

4 To shape the lip at the rounded end, Roehl installs a large pipe with rounded edges and works to continue the lip around the end. "The key is patience," says Rob. "People shouldn't try to do this too fast."

After the piece has the correct basic shape, Smith and Roehl decide to give it more of an edge, to make it stand up more off the tanks. So Roehl switches to a rectangular pipe in the vise and rolls the edge over that.

Rolling the edge to a sharper angle means the piece straightens out and must be "rolled" again. To help create the new, exaggerated lip Roehl uses a small shrinker that helps to give the piece the correct curved shape.

All that's required now is to roll the upper end a little more over a piece of pipe. In order to get the piece to roll down at the end of the tank, Roehl makes small pie-cuts along the lip and then bends the piece over another fixture. Then he welds up the little pie cuts after the piece has the right shape.

To mount the dash, Roehl will weld small threaded tubes to the top of the frame and then simply drill a small hole in the dash itself. Button-head Allen bolts screwed down into the threaded holes will hold the dash tightly in place.

5 Once the edges are rolled, Roehl starts to bend the dash so it will follow the contour of the tanks. Roehl likes to do as much of this by hand, rather than use the hammer. The idea is to move slowly and avoid going too far too fast.

6 Many trial fittings are necessary; here you can see the piece is coming along nicely, but Roehl and Donnie Smith decide it should stand up off the tanks more.

7 So Roehl uses a rectangular form to create more of a lip. The only trouble is that the new lip causes the piece to straighten out.

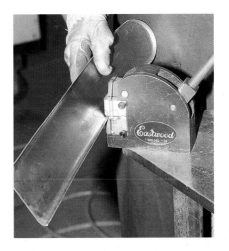

8 Roehl uses the more exaggerated lip to his advantage by putting it between the jaws of the small shrinker, causing the piece to pick up the curve needed to follow the top of the tanks. Small shrinkers like this (many also come with stretcher jaws) are available from Eastwood and other tool and hardware catalogs.

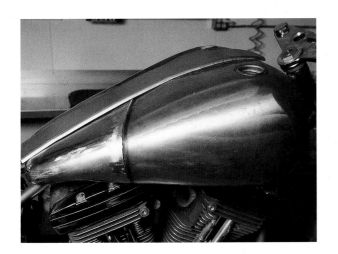

9 Here you see the results of the shrinking. The finished piece fits pretty well except for the end near the seat.

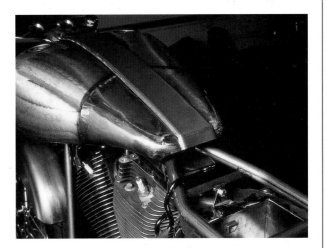

10 To bend the end, Roehl makes small pie-cuts with a tin snips and bends the edge down. The pie-cuts will be welded shut later. Mounting will be done by welding small threaded mounts to the top frame tube and then bolting the dash down with two small button head Allen bolts.

A CHAIN GUARD BUILT FROM SCRATCH AT METAL FAB

There's always more than one way to fabricate a part, and Jim Petrykowski from Metal Fab decides to show us an alternative way to create a simple sheet metal part.

The part in question is a chain guard, and though most people would make the part from two pieces welded together, Petrykowski decides to make this from one piece of sheet stock. To speed up our demo project, Petrykowski uses aluminum, though 18-gauge steel could be used as well. Jim starts with a sketch, then an exact drawing on poster board. After cutting out the template, the dimensions are traced onto two pieces of wood.

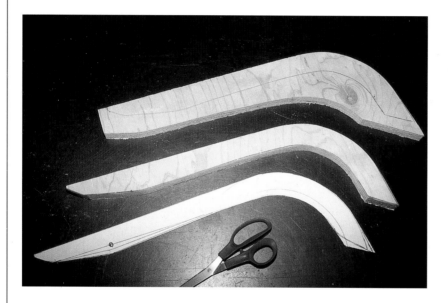

1 To make a chain guard from one piece of sheet metal, Jim Petrykowski starts with a two-dimensional template of the guard, which is used as a pattern to cut out two pieces of wood that will make up the hammer-forms.

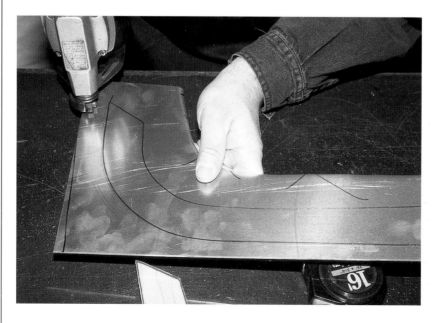

2 After drawing the side view of the guard on the aluminum and leaving enough material to form the top, Petrykowski rough-cuts the material with an electric shears.

Petrykowski uses an electric shears to rough-cut the aluminum, trims the edges by hand with a tin snips, and then clamps the piece between the two hammer-forms with enough material hanging out the top to form the upper surface of the guard.

Once the sheet stock is clamped between the two forms, most of us would start by hammering on the edge of the material. Petrykowski explains that there's a better way: "Traditionally, you start moving the material at the root. [Check the photos here for a better understanding.] That way the radius of the bend is smaller and you get fewer wrinkles. This is called 'corking.'"

By the time the bend has been created, there are some wrinkles along the edge. The wrinkles indicate that there is too much material, so some shrinking is in order. Petrykowski works the wrinkles with a soft-faced hammer, explaining that "The soft hammer actually cold-shrinks the metal at the point of the blows. A hard hammer used the same

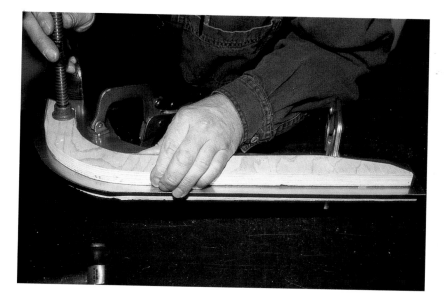

3 Next, the metal is clamped between the two pieces of wood.

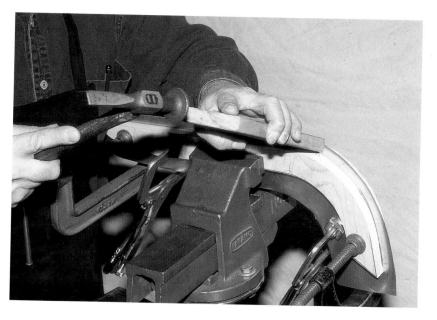

4 With the whole thing clamped in the vise Petrykowski starts the shaping. Note that he does not start the shaping at the edge, as logic might dictate, but at the base of the material where it emerges from the forms.

way in the same spot will simply further stretch the metal and turn a big wrinkle into four or five smaller ones. With the plastic hammer we can eliminate the wrinkle altogether."

At this point we have a roughly shaped piece just out of the forms.

With a piece of paper between the part and the bench for protection, Petrykowski clamps it to the bench and further finishes the rough edges with a hammer and dolly. Next he scribes a line along the edge to make it uniform, and then uses a tin snips to trim the edge. A single-cut file is used to further finish the edges.

Now he trims the inner edge to match the original mock-up. (He decides to leave it a little bigger than the original.) At this point, Petrykowski decides that the chain guard looks too "homemade," so he adds another dimension, a bead that runs along the center of the piece and helps the new part look more three-dimensional and professional. Finally, he makes a small dimple by stretching the metal over a small piece of pipe with a plastic hammer.

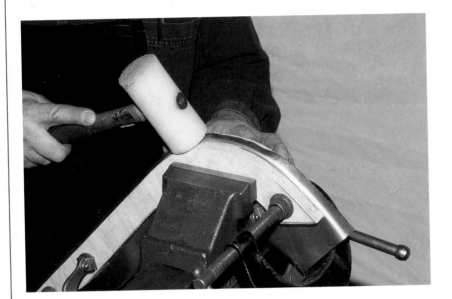

5 While the blows of a metal hammer would cause the piece to stretch, the hammering of the soft-faced hammer tends to gather the metal up. Petrykowski describes this as cold-shrinking the metal, which will eliminate the wrinkles.

6 Final clean-up of the edge is done with a hammer and dolly. This is really just a matter of straightening the edge. Note, there is a piece of light board under the piece so it doesn't get gouged by the surface of the bench.

Final Words of Wisdom

As we stand back for a look at the finished chain guard, Petrykowski passes on a bit of advice that might serve as a good overview of the whole process: "The part you build needs to fit the usage; it needs to be tastefully done. If you don't have a great idea, copy something that has the look you like. Make it work. Be sure that building the part is within your skill level. Don't start and get half-done and give up. Be sure the part has continuity with the rest of the bike. It must fit the bike; both literally and in terms of the design."

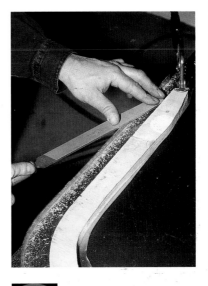

7 Petrykowski marks the inner edge, using a spacer to make a uniform line along the piece, and then does the final trim with a good tin snips.

8 A single cut file (which can be lubricated with bar soap) is used to finish the edge of the new chain guard.

9 To give the piece a more three-dimensional appearance, a step is rolled into the front surface. Different rollers can create a host of shapes including a concave or convex bead.

10 If you need a small dimple at the mounting point, stretch the metal with the help of a pipe or socket and a plastic mallet.

11 The finished piece; note the dimple. This chain guard was made from one piece of sheet metal, rather than two, which eliminated all that welding and finishing. With a little primer-surfacer and sanding this piece would be ready to paint.

CHAPTER 9 **CUSTOM PAINT**

Contents

Shop Safety 114

Set Up Your Shop 114

Sanders and Grinders 115

Air Compressors 115

Spray Guns 116

Inside the Paint Can 118

Powder paint:Good Looks
and Durabilityall from the
Same Process 120

Surface-Preparation
Materials 124

Space-Age Coatings 125

To Strip or Not to Strip? . .126

Surface Preparation 126

Paint the Easy Way—
The Harley-Davidson
Custom Paint Program . . .127

How to Spray Paint
in 250 Words or Less 128

Painting an Engine 128

Painting Case Study 130

There are a number of good custom painting books on the market (at least two of my own). So the intent here is to provide an overview of what's needed to do a basic paint job in your own shop. This chapter is intended to help the novice painter do that first paint job, and also help the non-painter speak intelligently with the professional painter.

Shop Safety

Safety is the dullest part of most technical books and the one section too many people skip over. The following comments regarding your safety in the shop have been kept short—in the hope that more readers will actually read them instead of skipping to the next chapter for some "real" information.

We tend to pooh-pooh safety warnings in the belief that we're too tough or that it can't happen here. The new miracle paints are better than ever, but part of the miracle has been achieved at considerable cost—cost in the form of high toxicity. Whether you only paint once a year or once a week, the chemicals can and will hurt you if you don't take the proper precautions.

The materials you need protection from include dust, paint, and solvent in both vapor and liquid form, and the isocyanate-based materials in both liquid and vapor form.

Always wear at least a good dust filter and eye protection during any work in the shop. The next step in protection would be a charcoal type of respirator used in all painting operations that do not involve isocyanates. You also need eye protection, either in the form of goggles or a full-face respirator that includes eye protection into the design of the respirator. Many painters wear special coveralls and rubber gloves during any painting operations. The gloves protect the wearer from having the chemicals enter through the skin, and the overalls also prevent your flannel shirt from contributing lint to the new paint job.

For spraying urethanes or any paints containing isocyanates, especially in a non-paint-booth atmosphere where the ventilation is poor, you need a hood or full mask supplied with fresh air from its own compressor. This equipment can be rented from many large rental companies so you don't have to pay out the big bucks on equipment that gets only occasional use.

Just a few more tips before closing. Don't use solvents and thinners to wash your hands or remove paint from hands and arms. Chemicals in the liquids are absorbed through the skin and end up in your bloodstream—so always use waterless hand cleaner or a similar product.

Finally, when you're spending hundreds of dollars outfitting your garage, spend just a few more and buy at least one good fire extinguisher and a smoke detector.

Set Up Your Shop

No matter how big your shop is, the work area must be well lit and have good ventilation. You need compressed air, heat if you live "up north," and plenty of electrical outlets. The shop needs a floor that can be kept clean, and access to running water is a nice bonus.

You need ventilation in the shop but you also need dust control during those periods when you're spraying paint. An easy way to provide ventilation of a garage is to open the door about a foot and use some Dustlok type of filter material, available from most paint jobbers, stretched across that opening. At the end of the door, slide in a ventilation fan pushing air out of the shop. Air drawn in will thus pass through the filter material, trapping any dirt.

The fan you use to push air out of the shop should be one designed specifically for that job, a fan that runs without any sparks at the brushes and no chance to ignite the flammable fumes often present in a painting shop. The flammability question affects your choice of heat, too. If you require heat, you may need a heater with a sealed combustion chamber or one approved for use in a shop. To repeat what was said in Chapter 7, gas and solvent fumes are usually heavier than air, so they fall to the floor. This means that flames or pilot lights must be kept as high off the floor as possible.

The point is, you need to be able to heat the shop up to a nice steady 70 degrees, minimum, without too much humidity, and without an open flame. Thrifty bikers often use wood heat for their garages, though it may not be a good idea when the building is filled with gasoline and flammable chemicals. Jon Kosmoski from the House of Kolor cites the too-cold shop as one of the most common reasons for the failure of paint jobs. You need a 70-degree shop not just during the actual painting but during the curing period as well.

It's not too hard to believe that the owner of this bike is a painter. The strength of Mallard Teal's design is based on the paint job, complemented by the bright accessories and the thorough attention to detail. Note the little things, like the caps used in or on all the bolt heads, and the painted eyes on the rear shock absorbers.

Sanders and Grinders

Because motorcycles are small, you don't need big, fancy grinders and sanders to do your body and paint work. You might want a small, air-powered grinder, but you certainly don't need the large grinders often seen in commercial body shops. As mentioned elsewhere in this chapter, big grinders with coarse pads create heat that warps and work-hardens the metal. Small grinding pad attachments that you can chuck into a 3/8-inch electric drill might be all you need.

A double-action sander, often called simply a "DA" is a very useful tool. Because the motor doesn't directly drive the sanding pad, which rotates instead on its own off-center pivot, the tool does a good job of sanding without gouging or leaving a sanding pattern in the filler material or paint.

Air Compressors

At the heart of the shop is the compressor, the one tool that dri-

ves so many others. The size of the air compressor you choose will depend to some extent on the type of paint gun you use (more on guns later). When it comes to buying air compressors, the old adage "bigger is better" definitely applies. Most paint manufacturers recommend you use a compressor with a minimum of 3 horsepower, but that minimum figure should probably be 5 horsepower, especially if you're going to use air-driven sanders and cut-off tools.

When looking at the cfm requirements of spray guns and shop equipment, you can use the guide of 4 cfm per horsepower; thus, a 3-horse compressor usually puts out about 12 CFM. Both the equipment you buy and the compressor you use to run that equipment carry a cfm rating. Pay close attention to these ratings when you shop for equipment.

When you consider buying a compressor, consider that the harder it works, the hotter it gets. Soon the air coming out of the com-

115

POWDER PAINT: GOOD LOOKS AND DURABILITY ALL FROM THE SAME PROCESS

Anyone who builds a custom motorcycle is concerned with both aesthetics and durability. We all want a bike that looks great and will retain those good looks even while we ride it day by day.

Not so very long ago most sheet metal and chassis parts were spray-painted, whereas engine parts were either polished or chrome-plated. Today, there's a new game in town, a means of providing both good looks and great durability in one process. That process is powder coating.

Powder coating actually got started after World War II, but only as an industrial process. In the past five to ten years motorcycle and automotive enthusiasts have come to realize how durable powder coating can be.

The photos shown here were taken at Best Coat in Blaine, Minnesota. Dick White, co-owner, explains that Best Coat has been in business for seven years and that motorcycle work makes up 50 percent of the company's business. Individuals looking for a good powder coating facility should ask

1 Cleaning and then thorough bead blasting was the first step for the cylinders and heads. Because these were polished, Dick White had to be sure all the polishing residues were cleaned off. Before applying the powder, White masks off gasket surfaces and areas where he doesn't want any powder. For the cylinders and heads, he uses a nylon cloth with silicone adhesive.

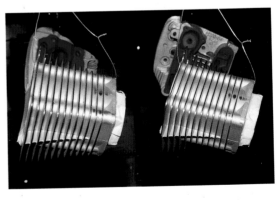

2 The fins on these cylinders and heads have been polished and will be "masked" later so we are left with black cylinders with shiny polished fins.

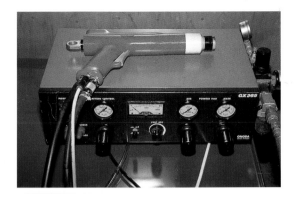

3 The control unit is used to determine the voltage difference between the part and the paint, and to adjust the air pressure moving through the gun. The gun creates a magnetic field that puts a charge on the powder as it leaves the tip.

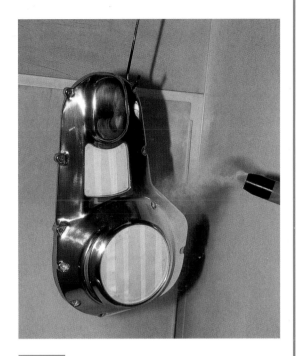

4 The primary cover has already been polished and then carefully masked off with a polyester tape that will stand up to the heat of the oven. The powder moves to the part in a slow-motion mist. Because this is a clear coat, it's important that the operator coat the part but put on no more powder than necessary—so the full shine of the aluminum comes through.

around with other bike or car enthusiasts to find a good shop. While powder coating seems at first like a pretty "brainless" operation, correctly coating the small irregular shapes that make up a motorcycle requires a tremendous amount of care.

Like any painting operation, the most important part of the powder-coating job is the preparation. A good shop must first remove, or have removed, all the old paint, dirt, and oxidation. Bead blasting is recommended, as is plastic blasting. Sand blasting, however, can leave the surface too rough (the powder will not "fill" the rough texture) and sand can be left imbedded in the parts.

White uses a dry polyester powder to coat the parts and reports that he can buy and spray everything from flat black to high gloss. A wide range of colors, including candies and even clear coats, are available. An electrostatic charge causes the powder to attach itself to the part being painted.

According to White, "The powder starts out in the hopper, where air pressure moves it through the lines to the gun. The paint gun itself creates the electrostatic field so the powder particles pick up a high negative charge. The part has a positive charge relative to the powder, the difference

in potential between the frame, or engine part, and the powder causes the powder to attach itself to the part's metal surface.

The "gun" used to paint powder doesn't really spray the material on the parts. Instead a soft cloud of material drifts up and onto the frame in an eerie slow motion. Because of the electrostatic attraction, the cloud of pulverized polyester wraps around the part. Paint that doesn't stick to the parts is drawn into the back of the paint "booth" where it can be collected later for disposal.

The electrostatic charge draws the material to the part, but what creates the bond between paint and part is the bake cycle that comes after the parts are coated. How long the pieces stay in the oven and at what tem-

5 Like spraying with liquid paint, the hard part is to get the paint up between the fins. White patiently works over the heads from different angles until he is happy with the coverage.

6 Waiting for the oven, these heads have been powder coated with gloss black. Instead of masking off the polished fins, White carefully wiped off the powder on the edge of the fins before the parts go to the oven.

7 After the parts are "powder coated," they go next to the oven, where temperatures approach 400 degrees. This is the step that actually causes the polyester material to bond with the metal.

perature depends on the size and material they are made from.

Almost any metal part can be powder coated, though the durability of powder coating often makes it an especially popular choice with engine and chassis parts. Before taking your parts to the nearest powder-coating shop White recommends that you keep in mind a few facts. "The parts you bring in will be baked in an oven. The heat is hard on seals or nonmetallic parts, so they

all have to come out first. And any oil in the pores of the metal will turn liquid and run, which can ruin the job."

Powder won't adhere well to chrome; the surface is so smooth and non-porous that the powder doesn't have anything to stick to. Powder will, however, stick to polished aluminum, as you see here. Even after polishing, the aluminum is still porous enough to give the powder something to stick to.

8 The finished heads and cylinders now have a very durable and glossy finish, which contrasts nicely with the polished fins.

9 The clear powder coat, applied over the polished aluminum, does cause a loss of gloss. Be sure to examine some samples of clear powder coating before having your polished parts coated.

For the purposes of the demonstration, we powder coated both the bright aluminum parts (some of which were seen in the polishing sequence earlier in the book) and also the heads and cylinders. While the bright parts received a clear coat, the heads and cylinders were done in gloss black.

The photos do a pretty good job of telling the story, though there are a few final notes. Even though a good operator will plug or mask off large openings and threaded holes, you will probably have to "chase" the threads on the frame you bring in. Likewise the inside of the neck, where the bearing races fit, may have to be sanded due to some accumulation of the powder paint. Also remember that "clear" powder coat isn't and will cause a loss of gloss. And as mentioned earlier, the paint won't stick to nonmetal parts so you can't use plastic filler to repair or mold any of the parts before powder painting.

Continued from page 119

paints have the metallic particles already mixed with the paint, or you can buy raw particles in various sizes and mix them with the paint yourself. Pearl particles are tiny bits of synthetic material added to the paint. The glow of a pearl job comes from the light that strikes the pearl flake and is then reflected to the viewer. The actual color you see depends on the color of the pearl particles, often acting in combination with the color of the base coat or the tinted clear coat.

Pearl paint jobs often react differently to different types and angles of light. Walking around a pearl job can be a little unsettling. From one direction you might see the blue base coat while from another you see the violet color reflected by the colored pearl chips (many painters describe this as flip-flop). A good pearl job has a lovely soft glow almost as though the light is shining through the paint from underneath.

New on the scene from House of Kolor and others are special "Kameleon" paints that change color very dramatically as you change the angle of viewing. Currently quite expensive, these new materials are sure to come down in price as they become more common.

Surface-Preparation Materials

The finest candy paint job in the world won't last long if the preparation and materials used under the finish paint aren't of the highest quality. First-time painters often think primer is just primer. Wrong. Primer comes in lacquer and two-part (often known as epoxy primer), as a sealer and as a primer-surfacer. Other materials, such as wax and grease removers and metal etchers are also needed to ensure that the paint you apply stays in place for years to come.

Wax and Grease Remover

Wax and grease remover isn't even a paint, yet it is the first thing you should use on the surface before applying any kind of paint. If it ain't clean, the paint won't stick—period.

Metal Prep

If you've stripped the tanks and fenders to their birthday suits, then you probably need to use a metal etch before spraying the first coat of primer. The metal etch prepares the bare metal for that first coat of paint. Though many shops spray epoxy primer over bare steel, many paint manufacturers recommend you treat the steel with metal etch first. Think of it as a primer for the primer.

Primer

A true primer is a paint material chosen for its good adhesion to the material it is sprayed over. Most provide good resistance to corrosion and moisture. A true primer is not meant to be sanded and contains a low percentage of solids.

Primer-Surfacer

Primer-surfacers are primer materials with a high solids content. While offering good adhesion like a straight primer, a primer-surfacer will help fill small scratches and imperfections, and sands easily. Primer-surfacers should be applied in two or three coats and then sanded when dry. If you fail to allow the material to dry properly before sanding, it will shrink *after* you've finished sanding, allowing small scratches (known as sand scratches) to show through the finish paint job.

Epoxy Primer

An epoxy (or two-part) primer like DP 40 from PPG or EP-2 from House of Kolor is a very durable primer material. These materials are known for their superior bonding abilities and great corrosion resistance. An epoxy primer is a good choice for motorcycle gas tanks, and will help prevent spilled gasoline from working under the top coat of paint and causing a blister around the fill cap. The catalyst in these paints (at least in the case of PPG and House of Kolor's products) is not an isocyanate, so most painters spray these materials with only a charcoal type of respirator. It should be noted that PPG recommends a fresh-air hood in spite of the fact that there are no isocyanates in these products.

Some of these like the EP-2 and KP-2 from House of Kolor can be sanded like a primer-surfacer, while others are meant to be used as a strict primer. Many of the two-part primers can be used as the sealer coat before the color coats are applied. Though they are durable and useful materials, each is a little different, so be sure to follow the manufacturer's recommendations.

Primer-Sealer

A primer-sealer, sometimes known as a sealer, is meant to seal or separate two different layers of paint. A coat of sealer is often applied as the final coat of "primer" before starting with the first of the finish coats. This is not a sandable finish, but is meant to seal two different types of paint. For example, lacquer sprayed over enamel will often cause a reaction between the two paints, so a sealer is applied before the lacquer is applied. (Enamel sprayed over lacquer isn't usually a problem, but a sealer should be used anyway.)

The other advantage of using a primer-sealer is to achieve good color holdout. Sometimes the final coat(s) of paint will soak into the primer coats underneath. This dulls and changes the color of the final coat. Color holdout means the top or final coats are "held out" and prevented from mixing in any way

SPACE-AGE COATINGS

Coatings That Aren't Chrome or Powder

Motorcycle builders are accustomed to having many of the parts on their bikes coated with various protective and beautifying materials. The outer primary goes to the chrome shop while the frame and swingarm make their way to the powder coating facility. Yet, there is another group of coatings that we are mostly unfamiliar with, despite the fact that these space-age coatings can help us build brighter, more functional motorcycles.

These coatings break down into three groups with very different properties: thermal barriers that contain heat, solid dry films to minimize friction, and high-temperature coatings that help a material to disperse heat.

The thermal barriers are actually ceramic, and ceramic matrixes, which act as an insulator to heat. Applied to a piston crown or the inside of a combustion chamber, these coatings will help contain the heat of combustion so more of that heat can be converted to horsepower. Jaye Strait from Britech in Southbridge, Massachusetts, explains that they often do more than just the pistons: "On a lot of bikes we coat the piston crown, the face of the valves, the combustion chamber, and the inside of the exhaust port. We do this for a lot of vintage bikes like Knuckleheads and for vintage race bikes. They run better and the oil temperature goes down significantly."

Solid, dry films are used to minimize friction. Applied to a piston skirt, the material helps that piston slide up and down in the cylinder with a minimum of friction and fric-tion-caused heat. Though people often speak of these films as being "Teflon-like" they actually have very different properties as compared to the stuff that's on the inside of your favorite frying pan. While no-stick cooking surfaces are designed to shed oil, these dry films, made up of a graphite mixture, act as a wetable surface that actually holds oil. To quote Jaye again, "When you look at a dry film under the microscope, you see a bumpy surface. The bumps help to minimize contact between the piston and the cylinder and also provide more surface area to hold an oil film—and there simply isn't anything much slipperier than oiled graphite."

When compared to ceramic coatings, the high-temperature coatings have the opposite attribute. Instead of insulating a part so heat is retained, these surfaces aid a part to give up heat to the atmosphere. An exhaust pipe or header with the high-temperature coating will not only look and resist corrosion better than a non-coated pipe, it will run cooler as well.

Motorcyclists have ignored, and been ignored by, most members of the coating industry. Jaye Strait says he went into the business because the majority of shops that offered the coating services he needed were geared to industry or the automotive market. Thus, when looking for a shop that can coat two pistons instead of eight, you need a facility that understands motorcycles. Ask around with the racers in your area or the vintage club to find a shop that understands the unique needs of motorcycle builders.

with the paint underneath. This means the Porsche Guards Red you spray on the tanks will look like and remain looking like the color chip in the paint book.

Adhesion Promoter

Adhesion promoters are similar in intent to primer-sealers and are sometimes used to ensure that one coat of paint will stick to the older paint underneath.

To Strip or Not to Strip?

As stated earlier, it's dangerous to spray lacquer over enamel, less so to spray enamel over lacquer. You may wonder whether the paint on your Harley is lacquer or not. Well, just take a little lacquer thinner to a hidden spot and see if it dissolves the paint. Before spraying over an old paint job, remember that no matter what type of paint it is, you can apply so many layers before the paint cracks.

What all this means is that when in doubt about whether or not to put more layers over an old paint job there's one simple answer. Don't. Strip the paint instead and start fresh. By stripping the paint, you eliminate all the hassles of compatibility and too many layers of paint. By working from bare metal, you control all the steps in the painting process and are thus better able to ensure success. You will discover and eliminate any old bodywork and start over fresh. By discovering and repairing any old repairs, you eliminate one more thing that might ruin your new paint job.

A Few Things to Keep in Mind

The new paints are better than ever, more durable and colorful than anything seen before, But there are, of course, just a few things you have to keep in mind.

Each manufacturer makes an information sheet available for each product. These sheets contain a wealth of information regarding the mixing, use, and application of the paint. Should you follow one light coat with a heavy coat? How long are the flash times? How long before you can apply or remove tape? All these questions and more are answered in the product information sheets.

Strangely, the safety information is not included in most of these information sheets, so you must rely on the labels on the cans or ask for the safety data sheets for each product.

Speaking of safety, be sure to use a charcoal type of respirator in any painting situation, except where isocyanates are involved, in which case you need a separate fresh-air system.

Most modern paints have evolved into "systems" designed by each manufacturer to answer a certain need. It's dangerous to spray lacquer and then use a urethane clear coat. If you're spraying acrylic lacquer, use lacquer for the base, candy coat, and final clear. Try to buy all the paint from one company—probably as part of their system. By using base coat, candy coat, and clear coat from one manufacturer you know all the paints are designed to work together and will be totally compatible.

If you have any questions about compatibility, be sure to ask the paint supplier. There's nothing worse than slaving over a great paint job only to have the paint wrinkle when you spray on the clear coat. Though primers and sealers are pretty universal, never use one company's catalyst with another company's paint.

Both House of Kolor and PPG make base coats that contain no isocyanates and can be clear-coated with either urethane or lacquer. By clearing these paints with lacquer, you can do a paint job at home that's free of any isocyanates and requires no renting or buying of a fresh-air system.

In order to do a successful paint job, you need to remember a few key rules of the painted road: Be careful with the preparation, use one type of paint from one manufacturer whenever possible, keep the shop at least seventy degrees, and read the directions—before you start painting.

Surface Preparation

Painting is one of those operations where the work you do before applying the paint has more to do with the outcome than does the paint application itself.

Jon Kosmoski is fond of the saying, "When you put your paint on over someone else's you're using their work as the basis for your own."

When in doubt, take it all off. Strip the parts to bare metal and start over.

Stripping can be done with chemical strippers, dip stripping, sand paper, or blasting methods. Each has advantages and disadvantages.

Blasting

The best-known blasting technique is sand blasting, definitely an aggressive method of paint removal. Though this mechanical process may work well for large, heavy objects, there are problems when sand blasting is used on sheet metal. First, the stream of sand propelled by high-pressure air hits the sheet metal with tremendous force, and that force and abrasion create heat, which often warps the sheet metal. Second, the pits created by the sand blasting stretch the metal, causing more warpage. If that weren't enough, the heat causes embrittlement of the steel.

Before telling you to never have the sheet metal parts sand blasted, I have to add that there are some sand blasters who understand the need for caution and can successfully sand blast sheet metal, but it requires an understanding operator.

Plastic blasting has become popular on a commercial scale and has evolved into a whole new industry. Less aggressive than sand blasting, this process can be used to remove paint without attacking and warping the metal itself.

The particles themselves are made from thermoset plastic, and each particle has sharp edges designed to cut paint without the need for high air pressure. The length of time it takes to strip a part depends on its size, the type of paint being removed, and the number of paint layers. This equipment runs on a high volume of relatively low-pressure air—20 to 40 pounds.

The plastic media is recycled, filtered, and used over again, until it gets too pulverized to cut the paint. In fact, new media is seldom used alone; some old media is usually mixed with the new in order to slow the cutting action. Because the old media and paint dust contain no toxic chemicals (the small amount of lead in some old paint pigments is considered insignificant), disposal of the dust is never a problem and helps to hold down the cost of the process.

When you consider the high cost, mess, and environmental problems inherent in chemical strippers, this new plastic blasting looks pretty good. It costs no more than chemically stripping a part, it's neater, safer, less toxic, and leaves no stripping residue in nooks and crannies where it can seep out later and ruin a new paint job. If you've got rust to deal with, this is not the best method. But if you're just trying to get off the old paint, then taking it to a shop that uses plastic media to remove paint makes all the sense in the world.

Chemical Stripping

A variety of paint strippers are available at the hardware or paint supply store that will allow you to strip the paint off those fenders. Anyone who thinks this process is easy (even on small parts) probably hasn't tried it yet. Chemically stripping even small parts is a time-consuming and messy operation that requires rubber gloves, an apron, and good ventilation.

Most of the strippers qualify as toxic waste. If you use very much of the materials you should take the time to dispose of them responsibly (see the disposal section at the back of the book). In order to avoid the disposal hassle, you might want to use one of the new, environmentally friendly strippers.

Each brand of stripper will have a slightly different set of directions—be sure to take the time to read them. Most recommend that you score the surface with a razor blade, for example, to help the stripper get under the surface of the paint and work faster. Most can be brushed on with an old paint brush. By moving the brush in one direction, the stripper will "glaze over" with an agent in the stripper that prevents it from drying out. If you brush back and forth, this anti-drying agent is rendered useless.

The paint stripper works best if you leave it alone and give it time to work—let the chemicals do the work. Two or three applications are often necessary and will still require some handwork with sand paper at edges and crevices after the stripper is all removed. Be sure to clean the parts thoroughly after the last coat of stripper and follow the directions with regard to any final flushing procedures. At the very least, wash the parts down with lacquer thinner or a similar cleanser so there's no lingering stripper to react with and ruin the new paint.

It's often a good idea to use a metal prep or metal etch agent prior to the first application of primer. Strippers usually leave steel in poor condition to bond with the first coat of paint. Again, each of these products is a little different. Some are one-step products and some require two steps. Take the time to read and follow the directions.

Sanding

Sanding is certainly a less-than-ideal means of stripping parts. It's time consuming, expensive, and dirty. It works reasonably well if the parts aren't too big, the paint isn't too thick, and there isn't much rust.

Though it sounds obvious, always sand with a pad no more aggressive than necessary and use a DA sander instead of a big grinder. When doing any kind of body work or sanding it's good to remember that large grinders create lots of heat (that work-hardens and warps the metal) and that a coarse pad creates grooves that need to be filled later.

In the end, the method you use to strip the paint from your tanks and fenders is going to depend on your pocket book, the resources available to you, and your own personal preference. Plastic blasting does a great job on paint while leaving the metal just as it was before the stripping started. Acid dips and chemical strippers pose a series of problems that make them less than ideal for all but small parts or special situations.

In the end you need to use a system that's neat and doesn't trouble your conscience when you stuff the remains in the garbage can. Pick a system that doesn't leave behind traces of chemicals that cause a paint failure later.

Paint the Easy Way— The Harley-Davidson Custom Paint Program

If all this sanding and spraying of lacquers and urethanes sounds like entirely too much work, consider the alternative, a complete paint job done through your local Harley-Davidson dealer.

George Edwards, from St. Paul Harley-Davidson, explained that the paint jobs are of the highest quality and the prices are very reasonable, but there are a few ground rules.

1. The parts you bring in to be painted must be genuine Harley-Davidson sheet metal. No aftermarket or custom parts will be painted.
2. You can specify any solid color or any combination of colors Harley has ever used. You can even specify an automotive color, for example, 1993 Chevy Lumina red.
3. The parts must be in very good condition, with all hardware removed; they will not remove trim or do bodywork on the parts.
4. You can use nearly any Harley-Davidson logo. Some old decals and logos that aren't in the accessory catalog are included in the custom paint program.
5. You can't, however, buy or use the special cloisonné logos unless you can prove you need them to repair an original bike that had those as standard equipment.
6. The Achilles heel of the program—slow turn-around time—is soon to be eliminated as a new paint facility comes on line.
7. Pricing is done in five stages, depending on the piece(s) and the complexity of the desired paint job.

So if you're looking for a painless way to have that sheet metal repainted, or if you want to buy a second set of painted sheet metal for the "convertible" effect, stroll on up to the parts counter at the local dealer and inquire as to the specific prices and necessary down time.

When painting, it is important to hold the gun 90 degrees to the object being painted. Move the gun in straight lines, don't follow the lines of the object when painting a gas tank or fender. Most paints call for a 50 percent overlap between each pass (as shown) though some candies and pearls call for a 75 percent pattern overlap. Be sure to read the tech sheets for each product; they're free and contain a wealth of information.

How to Spray Paint in 250 Words or Less

When you decide to fire up that paint gun for the first time, you need to remember the basics of spray painting. First, the gun must be moving when you pull the trigger and begin applying material. With a two-stage trigger, painters usually pull the trigger partway so air moves through the gun, start their hand moving, and then fully pull the trigger as the gun approaches the area where they need to start applying paint.

Second, always keep the gun 90 degrees to the object being painted. That way the paint goes on evenly. If the gun is tipped relative to the object, then the top or bottom of the paint fan will contain more paint than the other.

Third, always move the gun in straight lines across the object. Avoid the temptation to have each pass of the gun converge when painting tapered objects like a motorcycle tank. An object that combines flat panels with curves (think of a rectangular 1-gallon can

of lacquer thinner) will require that the flat panels be painted in a series of horizontal passes across each panel, combined with a "banding" pass up or down the curved section at the corner.

Fourth, unless the paint manufacturer tells you otherwise, each pass of the gun (as you work across a flat panel, for example) should overlap the last pass by 50 percent.

Painting an Engine

Painting an engine isn't difficult. Aluminum or cast-iron can both be painted in much the same way you would paint a fender or gas tank. If you can paint an engine, you can obviously paint a transmission in the same way.

The most important task is to get everything really clean. You also have to be sure to use the right primer for aluminum or cast iron. Of course, any primer you use should be a catalyzed two-part product like KP-2 from House of Kolor or a DP product from PPG. Because engines live in such a

Before each application of paint, it's a good idea to go over the object with a tack rag and compressed air to eliminate any dust on the surface. Most spray guns have a two-stage trigger, so by partially pulling the trigger the gun only puts out air and no paint.

harsh environment, exposed to heat and chemicals, only catalyzed urethanes are good enough to topcoat your automotive or motorcycle engine (though Harley-Davidson does make a special wrinkle black paint available at any parts counter).

If parts of the engine have been polished, like the edges of the fins, for example, you must be sure to get all the polishing materials off the parts prior to paint application. A good washing with hot water and dishwashing detergent is a good way to start, followed by a "final wash" or solvent that will not leave any residue behind.

Taping

Taping off the areas that you don't want painted is one of the most time-consuming propositions. For the fins you can either use very narrow tape, or apply 1/4-inch tape and then use an X-acto knife to trim it to exactly the right size.

You need at least one coat of primer, possibly two if you're trying to soften the roughness of the castings. Some painters carefully strain the primer to minimize the chance that there will be any bumps in the final coat of primer.

Applying the paint to a Harley-Davidson engine is difficult because it's hard to get the paint into all the

areas between the fins. Kosmoski recommends that you come in at the parts from various angles to be sure there aren't any areas that don't receive paint. "It's really hard to paint these engines," he says. "It's like the paint wants to blow back at you as you move the gun over the surfaces. You have to be careful to get good coverage over the entire engine."

Painting an engine is not magic, just another case of using the right materials for the job and following the correct procedures for those products. Use catalyzed urethanes over a two-part primer, skip the sealer, and be sure everything is squeaky clean before you start.

PAINTING A ROAD KING CONVERSION

The parts seen here are the same parts seen in the Road King conversion discussed in Chapter 9.

The work is done by the Wizard, Bruce Bush, in his shop just north of Minneapolis in Blaine, Minnesota. Though the focus here is on the paint job, considerable work goes into the tank and rear fender before the first coat of primer can be applied.

Before painting, Bush molds all the parts. That is, he applies body filler to low spots and areas where the tank was modified, sands the filler with 36 grit, applies another coat of filler, and then sands that with 80 grit. Next, he treats the remaining imperfections with a two-part glaze (a lighter filling material), which is sanded with 180 grit. Bush then applies three coats of two-part primer surfacer, which easily fills the 180 grit scratches. After block sanding with 180 grit, Bush applies more primer-surfacer

and eventually works his way to 400-grit sandpaper. The final application of primer is a single coat of DP 90 from PPG, which is used as a sealer in this application.

The base coat and all the colored materials used here are from the House of Kolor. The base coat, BC-25, is applied in two coats. Once the BC-25 is dry to the touch Bush sprays on the MB-01 Silver-White Marblizer. This material is sprayed on as a light mist; then the plastic wrap is applied while the paint is still wet and is allowed to sit for less than a minute before being pulled off, leaving a unique and very "marble-like" texture underneath.

The marblizer can be used in a variety of ways. In this situation the marblizer is only part of the paint job. Bush topcoats the marblizer with SG-100 intercoat clear, which is recommended when the marblizer is to be top-coated with a urethane, followed by three coats

of UK-8 Kandy Tangerine. Next he puts on two coats of UC-1 Kosmic Clear, sprayed wet on wet. He allows it to dry, and then sands with 600 grit.

After sanding with 600, Bush lays out a design free hand, with thin, 1/8- and 1/16-inch masking tape. Bush pulls the tape roll with one hand and then maneuvers the tape into position with the other. After the design is laid out he masks off the rest of the areas with 1-inch masking tape.

When the masking is done, Bush goes over everything with a tack cloth and the paint gun, using the gun (with the trigger pulled only partway) to blow off any dust. Next, he applies a coat of sealer, and as soon as the sealer is dry, the first coat of Orion Silver BC-02 is applied. Eventually, he puts three coats of silver down on the unmasked area. This silver is the base for the candy color to follow.

1 Here Bruce Bush uses a gravity feed, HVLP gun to apply the sealer, DP 90, a two-part primer from PPG that can be used as a sealer. As he paints, he keeps the gun 90 degrees to the tank and follows an imaginary grid of horizontal lines. The sealer color was chosen to be close to the color of the next coat, in this case the next coat is the BC-25 Black Shimrin base coat.

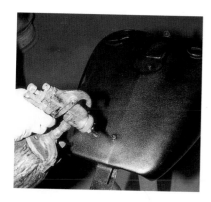

2 On top of the two coats of BC-25 Bush applies a single light coat of the marblizer. It's important to follow the directions for the marblizer; if you wait too long the material gets too dry to work correctly. The paint is applied with a Sharpe siphon-style high-pressure gun.

3 The plastic wrap is applied while the MB-01 Silver-White Marblizer is still wet and allowed to sit on the paint for 20 to 30 seconds. How you lay out the plastic wrap, when you put it on, and how long you leave it on—all will affect the final pattern and look. If you pull the wrap while the marblizer is too wet the paint will flow and change the pattern. Bush suggests you work with a test panel before doing the final paint, so there are no surprises.

4 After the marblizer dried, a single coat of SG-100 intercoat clear was applied, which will ensure the marblizer is protected from the urethane that is applied next. Here, Bush puts on the third coat of UK-8 Kandy Tangerine. Because this urethane is a candy color, the marblizer will show through the tangerine color. This Kandy Tangerine will be top coated with two coats of clear.

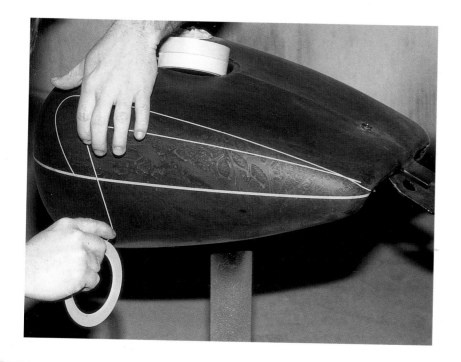

5 What you see here is the design of the art work being laid out free-hand with very narrow masking tape. Before laying out the design, Bush had to topcoat the Kandy Tangerine with two coats of UC-1 Kosmic Clear, which was allowed to dry and then sanded with 600-grit paper on a sanding block. All this had to be done before doing the art work because you can't sand on a candy color, but in most situations you have to sand the surface or the next layers of paint will not adhere.

On top of the silver, Bush sprays three coats of candy tangerine, the same color used on top of the marblizer earlier in the process. After pulling the tape and allowing the last coat of paint to dry, Ken Madden, resident pinstriper and airbrush artist, outlines the freshly painted pattern. The pinstripe paint Madden uses is special urethane striping paint from House of Kolor. The brushes are the odd-looking and very specialized brushes designed for pinstriping.

The final steps for this paint job are the six coats of clear applied after the pinstripes are dry, followed by block sanding with 600-grit paper, and then more clear coats so the final finish is extremely bright and very flat. After drying overnight, Bush block-sands all the sheet metal with 1500-grit paper and then finishes with a perfect polishing job.

6 After he likes the design, Bush masks off all the areas where he does not want any paint with 1-inch masking tape and masking paper. It's important to make sure the masking tape sticks at the edges so no paint can creep up under the edge and ruin the effect.

7 You begin to understand why these paint jobs cost as much as they do—after masking, the tank was painted with a sealer and three coats of BC-02 Orion Silver. The silver (which is a metallic) makes a good base for the additional three coats of Kandy Tangerine, which we see Bush applying here.

8 After the tape is pulled the tank looks like this. Note how the candy paint allows the marblizer and silver metallic to show through. Marblized areas are dull because they were sanded. The pinstripes come next and then the final coats of clear.

9 Pinstriping requires a variety of specialized products and tools. The most common paints are one-shot enamel or urethane striping and lettering enamel from House of Kolor. The four long-bristle brushes are designed to hold a large volume of paint so the painter can lay out a long line without the need to stop and dip the brush.

10 Ken Madden steadies one hand with the other while he lays on a perfect straight line. Part of the pinstriper's skill is understanding exactly how much to thin the paint so it flows out nice and even, without running and without any dry spots. Pinstripes act to clean up the paint edge and are also a big part of the overall paint design.

11 This close up of the tank top shows the finished paint. Note how different effects have been obtained with the same basic paint depending on how the plastic wrap was applied and removed.

Contents

Sportster 135

FX or Shovelhead 137

Chrome Plating 138

FXR 143

Softail 144

Polishing 146

Dressers 148

Dyna 148

How the Old-Timers
Did It 149

Bike Assembly Case
Studies 150

Bike Assembly
Case Studies 156

Most builders of Harley-Davidsons are not as skilled, talented, and experienced as Arlen Ness, Donnie Smith, or Dave Perewitz. Most of us are individuals of moderate skills and even more moderate budgets. This bolt-on chapter was conceived as an idea chapter. (Maybe they're all idea chapters)— ideas for individuals who don't plan to build a full-on custom bike.

The basic concept is simple— most of the good-looking custom bikes are really no more than a nice paint job combined in a tasteful way with some carefully chosen accessories. Because many of those accessories are chrome-plated, a portion of this chapter is dedicated to explaining what it is that creates the magic sparkle, the sparkle that never seems to go out of style.

Another portion of the chapter is devoted to following trends. What are people doing with their Sportsters, FXRs, Dynas, Softails, and dressers? The emphasis here is, again, on the newer models. What parts and techniques are people using to create their new bikes?

The discussion might be called a compendium of biased motorcycle journalism. This is not intended to be the definitive list of things that can or cannot be done to an FXR or Softail. This is more food

Give your Sportster the look of a Big Twin and help set it apart from the crowd with a new skirted fender and Fat-Bob-style tank from CCI combined with two-tone paint, early tank logos, and just the right accessories.

for thought. If you disagree with the ideas and opinions presented, that's fine. Maybe they can be a starting point for your own, very different, project.

A final note about common sense. Much of what we call customizing is really a matter of cleaning up the factory designs. This often involves removing the big factory blinker lights and replacing them with small, trim accessory lights. From a visual standpoint, the effect is often very pleasing though you have to remember that motorcycles are often invisible to the people who drive cars.

Many accidents occur because the auto driver simply didn't "see" the bike. When replacing the big ugly factory lights with slim, trim designs from Arlen Ness or Rick Doss, try to place them on the bike where they do the most good, and don't go to extreme lengths to minimize the size of the light because then you minimize its light output as well. If nothing else, be sure the brakelight and taillight you use are at least as bright as the stock light. Extra-bright halogen bulbs, which replace the standard, two-contact 1157 bulb, are available for those light assemblies that just don't throw as much light as a stock unit does.

The other thing you need to consider when buying and replacing lights is the DOT. Many aftermarket lights are not "DOT approved." You probably don't give a damn about the DOT, unless you live in a state with tough inspection laws, or you get pulled over by an overzealous highway patrol officer some night.

Trends and Bolt-On Goodies Sportster

It always seemed odd, considering the large number of Sportsters sold each year, that there are so few really nice customized examples. That situation has begun to change, although Sportsters are still very

This mini-Heritage is based on an Evo Sportster. Donnie Smith began the transformation by adapting a complete Heritage front end, including triple trees, to the Sportster chassis. The "Fat Bob" tanks are from Custom Chrome and the rear dresser-style fender was originally built for an FXR chassis. Custom bags from Iron Bags, done in a Heritage style, hide the shocks and make the conversion complete.

much a minority at most events.

A variety of factors are at work to change that situation. First, Harley-Davidson made a wise move when it expanded and redesigned the Sportster line just a few years ago. Second, more and more parts are available for Sportsters from each of the major catalog companies. You no longer have to fabricate parts for your Sportster or adapt accessories intended for Big Twins because the aftermarket offerings are substantial indeed. Sportster owners even have their own magazine now, including *Hot XL* from TAM Communications.

The reason for the relative shortage of customized Sportsters may be that until recently many custom parts haven't been designed for Sportsters. Or maybe by the time a person is ready to

build a really nice bike, he or she has moved up to a Big Twin. Whatever the reason, it seems a shame, as the Sportster is certainly a good-looking bike. Sportsters have a certain basic simplicity that provides a special appeal. There's nothing extra here, just an engine, gas tank, and two wheels. This is your basic motorcycle, well built and well proportioned. There's no reason this design can't be enhanced and improved upon.

Each year the major aftermarket companies have added Sportster accessories to their catalogs. Seats, exhaust systems, fenders, and gas tanks designed solely for the Sportster line fill the pages of catalogs from Chrome Specialties, Drag Specialties, Custom Chrome, and Arlen Ness.

If you want a Sportster with the look of a Big Twin, just bolt on a mini Fat Bob tank and "flipped" Wide Glide style rear fender. Add wider bars, leather bags, and the seat of your choice to complete the illusion. Some owners have even added Wide Glide triple trees or a complete Fat-Boy style front end to create what appears to be a Softail that was left in the microwave oven too long. Though it would hardly be a bolt-on bike, you can buy a complete Softail Sportster frame from Tripoli, complete with rubber mounts for the engine.

Because the basic Sportster has changed little in appearance over the last 40 years, an enterprising rider could combine the right seat, front fender, paint job, and accessories to make a late-model Sporty

Hardtails are hot. This one, built by Bob McKay, uses an aftermarket frame but otherwise the parts are mostly genuine Harley-Davidson—which keeps everything simple, easy to service, and relatively inexpensive.

Customized or detailed? This nice old Shovelhead uses extra chrome, great paint, and just enough modern accessories to enhance the bike's classic status.

Though it's more than a bolt-together bike, most of this bike's success and shine can be traced to the paint, nifty wheels, and extra chrome—all of which can be done without a major tear-down.

look like the first superbike—the legendary XLCH.

Closely related, the XLCR (Harley's cafe racer built during 1977 and 1978) also provides food for thought if you're looking for a direction to go with a Sportster project. Duplicating the exact look of the XLCR would be tough without a gas tank, though a cafe-style, late-model Sportster would be an easy thing to put together with parts scrounged at the swap meet and the Storz catalog.

The Storz catalog is a great source for Sportster owners (and Big Twin owners as well), with aesthetic and performance upgrades to convert your XL to a road-race or dirt-track special. Included in the catalog is a variety of tanks and tail sections to create the right look. And to ensure that your 883 or 1200 goes as well as it shows, Storz offer a variety of engine and chassis upgrades: Everything from a 1200cc kit with cams and adjustable

pushrods, to Mikuni carb kits, stainless high performance exhaust, and Ceriani fork assemblies.

Because a 1200 Sportster offers a very lively power-to-weight ratio, it's easy to simply use a "performance" theme as you upgrade your Sportster. Mike McAllister at M-C Specialties reports you can squeeze a 150 series tire between the sides of a stock swingarm by taking a little material off the caliper mount and then adding a spacer of the same dimension on the other side between the hub and the inside of the belt sprocket. Because the stock Sportster fenders are fairly narrow, Mike uses a factory Fat Boy rear fender. The Fat boy fender is wider than the stock Sportster item, but it fits after he grinds 1/8 inch off the inside of the rear fender rails.

Enhance the race look with a big tachometer, mounted to flat drag-bars and add braided hose

and first-class hardware to the rest of the bike.

If all the above sounds like too much, why not just stay with the basic Sportster theme, a less-is-more kind of bike? Add a nice paint job, some tasteful accessories, new bars, maybe a seat, and a few upgrades in hoses and hardware. You'll have a clean machine that didn't cost a ton of money. If it's a 1200, you'll have a fast machine as well.

FX or Shovelhead

What can a person say about customizing the older FX four-speed Shovelheads? It seems everything has already been done, from chopper-style bikes to pro-street, race-oriented machines. Even the factory has worked a thousand variations on these bikes.

What some builders are doing to the FX bikes is smoothing them out and making them look more contemporary. Starting at the rear,
Continued on page 142

came with five gears right from the very start.

The FXR frame carries the battery and oil tank inside the frame, which helps to create a much more streamlined machine when compared to the older FX-framed bikes. The wheel base on the FXR, at 64.7 inches, is just more than 2 inches longer than the 62.3 in wheelbase of the early Super Glides.

FXRs lend themselves to a long, low, racy look. Lowered, with perhaps a bit of extra fork rake, they tend to stretch out even more as they hug the ground. Potential builders have to remember that "lowering" is done both literally and by sleight-of-hand. By eliminating a sissy bar and adding graphics that flow along the length of the bike, you can lower the bike visually another 2 inches.

Though the look may be passé, a small Arlen Ness fairing looks good on a long FXR. Because the FXR line has been out for so long, and is currently out of production, it's hard to be really original when building an FXR. The key then for building an FXR seems to be the oft-repeated themes of simple, clean, and uncluttered.

With one-piece side panels (available from all the catalogs), a small front fender, 19-inch wheel in front, and a Ninja-style flush-mount gas cap, an FXR can be both beautiful and businesslike. These make the proverbial win-win bikes, fast and sexy, yet because of the rubber-mounted engines, bikes that can be used as daily drivers as well. With detachable bags and a small detachable windshield, an FXR makes a good "convertible" bike—one that offers a certain amount of protection on the long road to Sturgis, yet can be stripped down later to cruise in style.

An unusual combination is created by adding the aluminum headlight nacelle and light bar, normally seen on dressers, to the front of this Softail. Rear view shows tombstone taillight and dual exhaust. Note the Electra Glide logo on the front fender and early gas tank logo.

Softail

Perhaps the single best marketing move made by Harley-Davidson was the introduction in 1984 of the Softail. With a triangulated swingarm and the spring/shocks mounted under the transmission, the whole affair was designed to look like the old Hardtail Harleys. The Softail gave Harley-Davidson sales a jumpstart and created a lot of work for the customizing shops as well. Introduced as an extension of the then-current Wide Glide, the Softail—with Fat Bob tanks, a long Wide Glide fork, and a variety of accessories—started life as a factory-custom.

Though all Harleys seem destined for modification by their owners, the Softail seems especially well suited to men and women who want to build a motorcycle of their very own. With an engine solidly bolted into the frame and limited suspension movement, the Softail is perhaps not the road bike that an FXR or Dyna is, but when a bike looks this good, who cares?

When the Softail was introduced, there were only two models.

Today, the Softail frame is the basis for at least four separate families of motorcycles. The popularity of the machine and the tendency of Softail owners to personalize their machines means that the catalogs from the major aftermarket companies are filled to overflowing with accessories for the Softail.

Trying to make sense of all the modifications possible to all these bikes is a tall order, but here goes...

Let's start with the frame. The Softail frame is unique and the aftermarket companies have designed a variety of covers and accent panels. In particular, the vertical, cast-frame section behind the transmission can be completely covered in chrome or simply accented with small chrome plates that glue into the concave sections. KuryAkyn and most of the other aftermarket companies make nice little chrome covers for the end of the swingarm. These little numbers hide those unsightly axle nuts and allow the swingarm to come together in a nice, chrome accent.

If your goal is simply a more sanitary Softail, add a new streamlined rear fender (with subtle skirting on the side) mounted with new chrome fender rails from Arlen Ness or one of the other catalog companies that allow the fender to sit closer to the tire than did the stock fender. Now you probably need a new seat because of the lower fender height. Add a matching front fender, or one that works with the style of the rear fender, and paint to taste.

A whole host of aftermarket swingarms and suspension upgrades, many discussed elsewhere in this book, are available for a stock Softail chassis. These can be used to improve the ride or simply lower your Softail. When lowering, remember that these bikes start out in life with a chassis that's fairly close to the ground, so lower with care.

In more general terms, the Softail with its old/new look lends itself to either the nostalgia treatment or more modern creations. The chopper look is making a big comeback, and a Softail with a springer fork is a good starting point. Use a skinny 21-inch front wheel, high bars, early logos on the tank (still available from your local Harley-Davidson dealer), and fishtail exhaust. The hardtail look can be enhanced with a fringed seat to hide the frame/swingarm area and a bobbed fender with internal struts. For a similar but different approach you could use a simple flat fender mounted solid to the swingarm and a two-piece seat. Add a tombstone or side-mount taillight and finish with metal flake paint (with really big flakes).

You could build a simpler retro bike by combining early accessories with a 1950s paint scheme and a little judicious lowering. Take the low-buck approach and leave the frame black—most people won't notice. What they will notice are the bright 1950s paint

Built a few years back, this Springer Softail illustrates the art of getting maximum bang from minimal bucks. What makes the bike work is the bobbed rear fender, which in this case is mounted to the swingarm, not to the frame. Scalloped paint job was laid on right over the stock black paint. Ape-hanger bars are a very necessary part of the bike's theme. Though the factory frame is raked, the bike might make a better early chopper with the stock fork angle and a stubbier profile.

hues and the well-chosen chrome accents.

Just because the shocks are hidden doesn't mean you have to take your Softail backwards in time. The missing shock absorbers and overall look means you can use a Softail as the basis for the most modern of motorcycles.

Dave Perewitz is perhaps the master of this look. Up front there's a wide glide fork with a 19-inch tire mounted on a billet wheel. The bars are low, the headlight mounts to the lower triple tree, and the gas tanks are stretched. With some extra fork rake, the bike starts to stretch out and exhibit a look that would be hard to achieve with any other style of chassis. Use one of the kits mentioned in Chapter 4 to install a 150 or wider rear tire, housed under a wider rear fender mounted with clean, simple aftermarket fender struts.

POLISHING

The sequence shown here was done by Joe Deters at Deters Polishing in Blaine, Minnesota. The part in question is the outer primary from a certain well-known, well-worn FXRT. Follow along as the primary goes from old and oxidized to slick and shiny.

1 The proverbial "before" picture. Note the discolored, dark aluminum. The small drain plug in the bottom of the cover was stripped and stuck, until Joe Deter took it to Metal Fab next door where they warmed it to 150 degrees (definitely not red hot), rapped on it with a hammer, and then worked it out by using a hammer and a blunt chisel.

2 Before the polishing starts, everything needs to be clean. You can make points with the polishing shop by washing everything thoroughly before you bring it in. After the cleaning, Joe takes the bead blaster to the recesses and screw indentations to make sure there is no remaining lacquer coating (some aluminum parts have a clear coat to eliminate oxidation) left on the parts or in the screw indentations. Joe uses glass beads not silica sand, which is too coarse and will become imbedded in the aluminum.

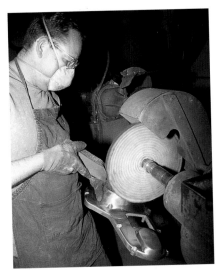

3 The polishing starts with a 240-grit belt. Oddly enough, Joe says this cover isn't a "bad one." Because it doesn't have any deep gouges in the aluminum—which would require a 120-grit belt as the first step.

4 Joe puts Tripoli compound on the cotton wheel coated with a greaseless compound and goes over the primary cover again, concentrating on areas that were hard to reach with the belt.

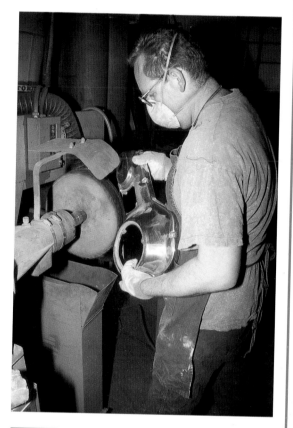

5 For the next step, Joe switches to the buffing wheel, which is well used and actually contains bits of aluminum from past work imbedded into the material. To this matrix is added more Tripoli compound, the actual cutting is done by both the Tripoli and the old aluminum working together. As the cover is held up against this wheel the bright lustre of the aluminum starts to shine through.

6 If this part were going to the chrome-plating shop, Joe would be done now. But it's not, so he moves to the color buffing wheel, which is coated with coloring compound. The coloring compound will bring out all the lustre and color of the aluminum. Before picking up the cover Joe puts on fresh gloves, which are dipped in flour, to absorb any skin oils that might stain the aluminum.

7 The finished product, which took more than an hour from start to finish. As Joe explains the process, the best work is the result of never using anything more aggressive than 120 grit, and making sure each step fully removes the sanding marks left by the step before.

A "fat" look is also often seen on Softails these days. This package requires a 16-inch wheel on each end, big wide fenders (perhaps the tail draggers from Arlen Ness or the Street Sweepers from Paul Erpenbeck), 5- or 6-gallon Fat Bob tanks and bars wider than the horns on a Texas Longhorn. Complete the look with a great paint job and a pair of long, straight pipes that run side by side all the way to the end of the rear fender.

In a design sense, the Softail may be the most versatile of the Harley-Davidson frames. Able to go backward or forward in time, this chassis can be used as the basis for a tall, stubby chopper or a long, lean roadster.

Dressers

There seem to be more and more custom dressers on the streets each year. Maybe it's the baby boomers getting older and going slower with more comfort. Perhaps the FL family of bikes is finally getting the recognition it deserves as the classic American road bike. The immensely popular Road King, with missing Tour Pak and signature FLH headlight nacelle, is certainly part of this trend.

The dresser phenomenon seems to be subtractive-customizing. That is, modify and simplify the bike by taking things off. Dressers have a very nice classic look all their own. By removing some of the factory-installed chrome trim and bobbles, the bike's natural good looks emerge.

If you're going to keep the handlebar-mounted fairing, take off as many lights as possible and mount the turn signals flush into the outer edges of the fairing. Drag Specialties and others offer rearview mirrors that mount just inside the corners of the fairing. Clean it up further by removing the trim from the classic front fender, or order one without any

A bright, modern dresser. Front turn signals are flush-mounted into the fairing while the rear blinkers are flush-mounted in the bags. Note the Fat Boy front fender, polished factory brakes, and detailed-to-death V-twin.

holes at all from your local dealer.

In back, a variety of companies make "fill-in" trim pieces that fit between the bags and the fender and make the bags seem more like an integral part of the bike. For the really trick approach you can flush-mount the blinkers into the trim piece between the bag and fender or simply remove the factory light bar in back and mount a pair of oval Rick Doss accessory lights between the bag and the fender.

For the low-and-slow crowd, bringing their dresser closer to the pavement is easier than ever, with kits from White Brothers to lower the back end without buying shocks or flipping the swingarm (the neat trick people were using to lower the back of a dresser up until the new kits came out).

If you're slowing down as you get older, don't worry. It's O.K. as long as you keep moving. And with the wealth of accessories available for the dresser chassis, you can now have your comfort *and* your style. Cruisin' in comfort was never so easy.

Dyna

Oddly enough, the Dyna line is similar to the Sportster group in the sense that the number of customized Dynas is rather small. Up until recently there weren't very many parts available for the Dyna, and whether that is the cause or effect of the customized shortage is a matter for debate.

Dynas mount the battery out in the open on the bike's right side, almost like an old Shovelhead. Donnie Smith streamlined a Dyna in his shop recently by making a wraparound cover that looks like an oil tank. It's a neat trick; unfortunately, it's hardly a bolt-on operation. In order to have room for a nice, sleek cover, Smith used a smaller battery from a Yamaha Royal Star, angled into the bike so they could make the cover as narrow as possible. "On the other side we moved the coil forward and got that out of the way," he explains. "But we had to fabricate the side covers and we also had to do some welding to get the battery box mounted correctly."

Before complaining that there aren't any accessories available for your Dyna, check out this bike from Bob McKay. Rear fender with "frenched" struts is available in two styles and two widths. Dagger front fender is available to fit most Wide Glide and narrow-glide forks and is made from new composite glass for good strength and flat sides.

The Arlen Ness catalog offers a simpler side cover that does bolt on, though it isn't as sleek as Smith's fabricated "oil tank." But there's another problem, because the Dyna frame changed in the area right under the seat in 1996, so the covers only fit the 1995 and earlier models.

In the good-news department, there is an emerging group of aftermarket parts available for the Dyna line. Originally developed by Bob McKay and offered through the Drag Specialties catalog, there are two rear fenders built strictly for the Dyna. These fenders have recesses to "French in" the fender struts. In Bob's words, "They give the bike a nice fat look. The strut is in the same place, so you don't really gain any clearance for a real

wide tire, but we've been putting in a 140 tire, and with the new fender the whole back of the bike takes on a wider look."

Among the growing pile of Dyna parts is a group of accessories and lights. To brighten up the left side you might add a chrome electrical panel cover and/or chrome belt guards, available from all the major catalog companies. In the hardware department, new high-quality axle adjusters are available, as are small accessory lights designed to mount to the swingarm.

The relative shortage of parts is sure to change as more and more Dynas populate the street. Until that happens, you just have to do a bit of adapting as you customize your Dyna. Almost like in the old

days—before there were big catalogs filled with parts.

How the Old-Timers Did It

Before there were Dynas or catalogs full of parts, bike owners customized their machines with their own ingenuity and by making and adapting the parts they couldn't buy. If your problem is how to customize a Dyna or how to do something original with a Softail, you would be wise to remember those early pioneers. Just because the fender you want isn't in the catalog doesn't mean it's an ugly shape or a bad idea. The men who lead the industry didn't get there by being timid or copying the factory. They achieved success with persistence, skill, and by trying new ideas.

BIKE ASSEMBLY

The case studies that follow offer a different perspective on this whole bike-building business. Instead of telling you about available parts or offering styling ideas for various bikes, this is an opportunity for readers to visit two shops and see how the professionals do their work.

The first example is a complete makeover for a 1987 FXR in the shop of well-known customizer Donnie Smith. Case study number two is a less complex operation, a conversion from dresser to Road King in the M-C Specialties shop.

Both are examples of real-world customizing projects. Note in the text the attention to detail displayed by the mechanics as they assemble these two bikes.

Screamin' Yellow FXR at Donnie Smith's Shop

The bike you see here started as a 1987 FXLR. The photos and copy will document the assembly of the bike, from the major decisions to the little things, like which nuts and bolts to use.

What's already been done as we start this sequence is the frame modification, which includes the addition of a new front section to the stock frame (known as a "hardhead"). The new front section adds a 3-inch stretch to the frame and gives it a final rake angle of 38 degrees. After the tubing was welded in place, Greg Smith molded both old and new welds and then sent the finished piece to Jerry Scherer of Lindstrom, Minnesota, for the paint.

The swingarm is left with its

1 In the beginning there was a frame, an ordinary FXR frame except for the new front section that gave the frame a 3-inch stretch and a final rake angle of 38 degrees. Completely molded by Greg Smith, the frame was then painted bright yellow pearl with House of Kolor paint. Note the swingarm with the very sanitary lower shock mounts.

stock dimensions, though the stock shock mounts have been replaced with cleaner mounts, and the whole thing was molded to match the frame. Don Tima, the mechanic doing the assembly, checks the fit of the swingarm on the rear transmission mount before installing the swingarm. Tima moves the cleve blocks (or bushings) in the swingarm over slightly so the swingarm will slide over the transmission mount.

Installation of the transmission is next, and Tima starts by first placing plenty of anti-seize in the hole in the rear tranny mount. The anti-seize will act as a lubricant and ensure that the bolt will still be removable two or three years from now. Before going any further,

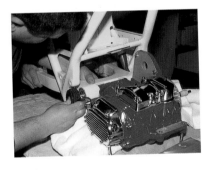

2 The FXR chassis uses a three-point engine mounting system. The rear mount is also the pivot for the swingarm. Here Don Tima and Roehl put the pivot bolt through both swingarm and transmission and get the outer bushings in place before bolting on the pivot end caps. Blankets and towels have been laid out to protect the freshly painted frame.

Tima puts duct tape on the inside of the frame rails to prevent chipping the paint during the installation. While Tima holds the swingarm and tranny together, Rob Roehl, another of Smith's crew, puts the rear mount bolt through and gets the outer bushings in place.

Before bolting on the swingarm caps, Tima cautions other builders, "The bolts for the swingarm caps are like grade 8 and they're chrome; they have a reputation for going halfway in and then stopping. So you have to be sure to use a tap to chase the threads on the frame and use anti-seize on the bolts." Next, Tima bolts the front motor mount loosely into the frame and then runs a tap through the threads on the chrome-plated engine bracket.

We should note here that all the bolts used to assemble the bike are grade 8 chrome-plated bolts from Gardner Wescott. Even the washers are hardened. That way they don't distort under pressure, which causes the chrome to flake off.

After once again protecting the paint on the frame with duct tape, Tima and Roehl set the engine in the frame. The motor that the boys install is what you might call a "hot rod 80"—80 cubic inches of free-breathing V-twin with shaved heads for a compression ratio of 9.5:1, a Crane 1000 camshaft, and a Super E carburetor from S&S. The ignition is the HI-4, also from Crane.

This is an engine that's as hot externally as it is internally. The bright red urethane paint is from House of Kolor, applied again by Jerry Scherer. The red contrasts nicely with the polished fins and chrome-plated rocker boxes. Of note: Though it may look like this

3 After the engine is installed and bolted to the transmission, the inner primary cover can be installed. When the engine and transmission were painted, the area where the two bolt together was left in bare aluminum. As stated earlier, if the inner primary doesn't just slide right on there's something wrong with the way the engine and transmission are bolted together. Note, the starter and shift shaft are already in place.

4 Don Tima installs the factory primary drive as an assembly, then the compensator sprocket, and the nut for the transmission shaft (which is left-hand thread).

bike has no oil tank, it actually carries one of Smith's modified tanks, which is taller than stock and lacks the big signature FXR bulge. The idea is to create an oil tank with the same capacity, but one that "opens up" the look of the bike.

Next, Tima assembles the clutch assembly and then prepares to install the inner primary. First, though, he puts new seals in the inner primary, for the shift lever, transmission, and starter, and installs the inner shift lever. Then he puts a little silicone on the back side of the inner primary and slides it into place, explaining as he does, "You can't ever force the inner primary up against the engine. If it doesn't want to slide into place, loosen and reset the connection between the engine and tranny; then try the fit of the inner primary again."

Tima puts anti-seize on the bolts that fasten the inner primary to the engine and transmission, and locks each one in place with the factory lock tabs. Next, he hooks up the ground strap between the engine and frame, necessary because the engine can't ground through the rubber mounts and heim joints. At this point the starter, complete with new brushes, is installed.

Before installing the primary drive Tima wipes off the transmission shaft and applies a good coating of grease on the engine shaft. Now, the compensator nut and clutch hub nut are installed and tightened to the correct torque specs (be especially careful with the clutch hub nut; if it goes on too tight it can split the hub), with Loctite on the hub nut.

5 The neck bearings are tapered rollers, which have been packed with waterproof grease. Note the small hole in the upper tube for the wiring to run through.

6 Tima installs the 39-mm fork tubes into the billet GMA triple trees. These tubes have been cut 2 inches and reassembled with Progressive springs. Note that the lower legs are painted rather than plated.

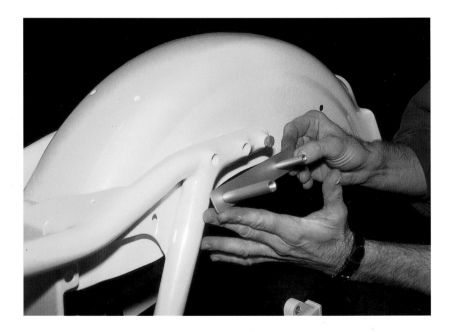

7 These are the fabricated brackets used to locate the rear fender and provide an upper mounting point for the shock absorbers.

The next part to come together is the front fork and triple trees. The trees are billet aluminum and come from GMA. The tapered neck bearings are packed with grease, much as you would pack automotive wheel bearings. Tima likes to use waterproof grease from Bel Ray just in case any water ever seeps into the neck.

The custom-made bars with the integral risers and speedo housing are attached next, with new bushings in the upper triple tree. Then it's time to insert the fork tubes and tighten the triple tree pinch bolts. The fork tubes are the standard 39-mm tubes used on later FXRs, cut 2 inches and supported by Progressive springs.

The front wheel for this bike is a combination of chrome-plated steel rim, chrome-plated spokes, and a steel hub, all assembled at Kokesh MC Parts. A GMA rotor attaches to each side and the hub is equipped with new wheel bearings and new seals.

The rear fender is mounted with the standard fender struts and special fabricated brackets that come through from inside the fender and thus leave no bolt head or nut on the inside of the fender for the tire to rub up against. These special fabricated brackets also provide the upper mount for the 11-inch Works shock absorbers. Though these brackets were made in the shop, Custom Chrome makes a similar bracket.

The rear tire is a 150/80x16-inch Avon. "A 150 on a stock rim is the widest you can go," explains Smith, "if you want to keep the stock swingarm and fender. On this bike we left the engine and

8 The fender and taillight are installed and Tima gets ready to slide the rear tire and wheel in place. The rear tire is a 150/80x16 inch Avon mounted to a 3-1/2-inch rim, which according to Donnie Smith is about the widest tire you can use with a stock swingarm and fender.

9 The factory manual shows exactly how to make a tool like this one, used to measure the distance from the swingarm pivot to the axle on each side.

transmission in the stock location and used one of our kits to install the wider rear tire."

The Donnie Smith kit typically consists of a machined caliper mounting bracket and a spacer (as described in Chapter 4) that mounts between the rear wheel pulley and the hub. Essentially, this moves the wheel to the right while the pulley stays in the stock location. Because this bike uses a GMA caliper and bracket, Smith takes material off the caliper mounting bracket and then takes half that amount off the inner bushing used to locate the caliper relative to the bracket. In this way the tire moves to the right and the caliper itself is centered over the rotor.

Before installing the custom taillight lens, Tima sprays the inner housing with silver paint in order to keep the light as bright as possible. The lens and bracket all come in from behind, Tima puts a little silicone on the edge of the lens before sliding it into position and bolting in the entire light assembly. JB Weld is used to secure the wiring harness for the taillight up into the corner of the rear fender. The horn for this bike is hidden down below the battery box where it's out of the way yet meets all legal requirements.

With the rear fender in place, Tima installs the rear wheel, the rear caliper mount, and bushings, as described earlier. Even the axle used in the rear is a nifty Donnie Smith design with flush-mount ends.

For the initial rear wheel alignment, Tima sets the wheel in place by eye and adjusts the belt to the correct tension. With the rear wheel up off the hoist, Tima rotates the wheel in the forward direction (don't worry if the belt crowds to

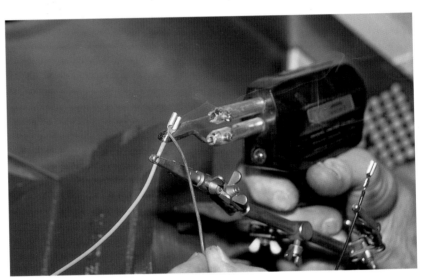

10 The 19-inch front tire, mounted to a steel rim, is mounted to the lower legs with a special Donnie-Smith built flush mount axle and ends. The rotors are from GMA, and though they've been plated, the outer area was left rough to provide the pads with a good friction surface.

11 The wiring harness used on this bike is fairly raw, and requires the installation of connectors like this one. All the ends are soldered in place and then shrink-wrapped. If you haven't wired a bike before, it's a good idea to ask for help.

one side when the wheel is turned backwards) and watches that the belt stays in the center of the rear pulley and doesn't crowd to one side of the rear wheel pulley. After he is happy with the way the belt runs he goes through the full driveline checkout procedure as outlined in the factory service manual.

Next, Tima mounts the Bub "Step Mother" pipes, which install with no gaskets but use bronze sealing-rings instead. Tima hangs the pipes loosely to see how all the brackets line up, then snugs up the brackets, does the final tightening of the flanges, and then the final tightening of the brackets.

The wiring harness used on this bike is from Drag Specialties, designed to fit many Big Twins from 1982 to 1994. This harness is cheaper than a full factory harness and uses all the correct color codes, but does not have the big plug-ins for the subharnesses already installed.

Note: The regulator, which is mounted in the air dam, grounds through the chassis. For this reason you must use a star washer under the mounting bolts or the regulator won't ground and regulate correctly. Now, Tima can finally set the gas tank on, carefully sliding it into the special front mount, which requires no bolt.

The gas tank on this yellow rocket started life as an FXLR tank, before Roehl stretched it to fit the new stretched frame and installed the flush-mount gas cap from CCE. In order to ensure that no seams leak in the tank, Smith sent it to Tank Renew, a company that bakes a synthetic liner into modified tanks like this one.

At this point, the bike is essentially finished. Final details include the seat, which is built from a custom seat pan (seen elsewhere in this book) covered by seat builder Keith Nybo. All the wiring runs inside either the frame or the handlebars. As mentioned earlier, the bars themselves were built in-house by Donnie Smith.

This FXR is a bike built to look good, yet remain the kind of bike that can be ridden on a regular basis—a custom motorcycle that succeeds in being both good looking and fully functional.

12 Detail shot shows the harness as it emerges from the frame. The ignition switch is mounted in the Dave Perewitz coil bracket, though there's a plug-in connector behind the bracket so the coils and ignition switch can be quickly removed for engine service.

13 The finished piece. With nice lines and great yellow paint this bike looks good at 10 feet. But it's also a machine assembled with enough attention to detail so it looks almost better when people get in close to scrutinize each fitting, bolt, and seam.

ROAD KING CONVERSION AT M-C SPECIALTIES

Dressers, Road Kings in particular, are enjoying immense popularity. All this attention caused M-C Specialties (outside Minneapolis, Minnesota) shop owner Mike McAllister to wonder just how hard it would be to convert an older dresser to full Road King status.

What started as just an idea turned to steel and chrome when a 1993 FLHTC came into McAllister's shop to be repaired after an accident. The bike had to be pulled apart and repaired anyway, and the owner wanted it "fixed up." So why not leave off a few things like the big fairing and tour pak, and add a few others like the Road King headlight nacelle and some nice customizing touches.

"The key to the whole thing is the installation of the correct Road King upper triple tree," explains McAllister." Other than that it's really a matter of stripping the bike and buying Road King parts. You need a Road King gas tank and ignition switch, then just extend the stock wires to the new switch and hook them up."

Though the conversion could be simple, McAllister went considerably beyond the original concept. After pulling the bike apart he ordered a new Fat Boy rear fender and FL style front fender, both from Harley-Davidson. After a trial fit, the rear fender was modified to accept a cat's eye taillight mounted nearly flush with the fender's surface. The stock light bar and turn signal assemblies

 Where it all started, with a stock 1993 FLHTC full-dress Harley-Davidson. Hard to believe, but under all that stuff is a relatively svelte and very modern Road King.

2 The key to the whole deal is the upper triple tree. Shown is the original dresser tree, which has been replaced with a Road King triple clamp. By using the correct part, the correct headlight nacelle and ignitions switch/fork lock can be used.

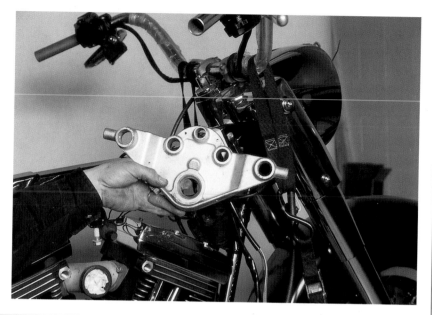

3 Though you could use the stock front fender, Mike McAllister chose to buy a new FLH fender from Harley-Davidson. Headlight nacelle is the original Road King piece from Harley-Davidson. Lower legs and chrome "cans" are original dresser pieces.

were discarded at the same time. In their place McAllister purchased fill-in sheet metal parts that mount between the bags and the rear fender. Small oval accessory lights, used as blinkers in this case, were mounted into those panels.

All the metal fabrication done on this bike is the work of Brian Mosbeck from Blaine, Minnesota. In addition to the modifications done on the rear fender, Mosbeck did some major massaging of the gas tank in order to get it to fit the bike and accept the dash and gauges. As McAllister explains, "The easy thing would have been to use the Road King gas tank, but we decided to use an FXR gas tank with the gauges mounted in the center."

Mosbeck built the sheet metal dash from scratch so the two Harley-Davidson gauges would fit the new tank. Because this bike uses a mechanical speedometer (late-model Harleys use an electronic speedometer driven by a magnetic pickup in the transmission) routing the speedometer cable could have been a problem. This problem was solved, however, through the use of an FXRS speedometer with a built-in angle drive that allows the cable to come in at the front of the tank.

The rest of the assembly and finishing of the bike was pretty straightforward. The new upper triple tree allowed McAllister to bolt on the factory Road King headlight nacelle. In order to get the big boat a little closer to the ground, White Brothers kits were used at both ends. In front, the stock springs were replaced with shorter, more tightly wound White Brothers replacements, while at the rear the shocks were relocated

4 Here you can see the fill-in sheet metal, available from Drag Specialties, and the way small oval accessory lights have been flush-mounted to make turn signals. Brian Mosbeck did the metal work necessary to install the Cat's Eye light in the Fat Boy fender.

5 The converted and customized Road King complete with marbleized candy paint by Wizard Studios in Ham Lake, Minnesota. *Mike McAllister*

with kits from the same company.

Before all the new parts were bolted to the converted king, everything went out to the Wizard's shop for the candy and marblizer paint job seen in Chapter 8. The finished bike shows what you can do with a little imagination and some clever parts swapping.

Either Way

In the end it doesn't matter whether you're updating an old iron-head Sportster or building a bike from scratch. Like these two builders, you need to start with a good concept, turn that concept into a concrete plan, and then follow through with careful execution.

It doesn't matter whether your plan calls for spending $800 or many thousands of dollars. If the idea's a good one and you follow through with the right team of mechanics and painters, you're sure to end up with a much-improved bike that you can call your very own.

Accuspray HVLP, 117
Aerocharger turbo kit, 57
Air compressors, 115, 116
Akront rims, 43
Andrews camshafts, 59
Arlen Ness Big Wheel conversion kit, 32
Arlen Ness calipers, 36
Arlen Ness chrome fender rails, 145
Arlen Ness Taildragger and Cafe fender
    designs, 96
Arlen Ness twin shock frame, 19
Arlen Ness Wide Tire Softail kits, 341
Arlen Ness, 34, 46, 134, 135
Avon tire, 35, 47–49, 153
Axtell cylinders, 92
Best Coat, 120
Bolts, 14
Brakes
    buying brakes, 31, 34, 35
    fluid, 38, 39
    hoses, 38
    pads, 36–38
Buchanan spokes, 43
Bush, Bruce, 130–132
Buttera, Lil' John, 40
Camshafts, 56–60, 71–73
Carburetors, 50–55
Carl's Typhoon carburetor, 54
CCI solid-mount swingarm frames, 20
Chrome plating, 138–141
Chrome Specialties, 10, 30, 31, 34, 36, 135
Clemens, Lee, 65–67
Coddington, Boyd, 40
Constant velocity carburetor, 51
Craig Walters accelerator program, 61
Crane-HiRoller camshafts, 60
Custom Chrome RevTech Accelerator II
    carburetor, 54
Custom Chrome, 30, 34, 96, 135
Cylinder heads, 92–95
Cylinders 91, 92
Davis, Steve, 99, 101, 105
Delkron cases, 87, 88
Departure Bike Works, 65
Deters, Joe, 146, 147
Disassembly
    how far to go, 13
    preparation, 12
Doss, Rick, 96, 135
Drag Specialties rims, 42
Drag Specialties, 30, 34, 96, 135, 155, 158
Dunlop tires, 41
Durkin, Ron, 118
Dyna 148, 149
Edelbrock cast heads, 93
Edelbrock QwikSilver 2 carburetor, 54
Edwards, George, 44, 91, 128
Engine cases, 87–91
Evolution engines, 58
Fat Boy front fender, 96, 142, 148
Fat Boy rear fender, 101, 137, 158
Fat rear tires, 30–33
Fat-Bob-style tank, 97, 98, 102, 105,
    134–136, 142, 144
Feuling four-valve cast heads, 93
Fitzmaurice, Dan, 92
Flywheels, 91
Frames
    Hardtail 17, 18
    molding, 22–25
    painting, 24, 25
    rake, 16, 21
    Softail, 16, 17–20

    stretch, 16, 21
    Twin Shock, 17–19
Frontdragger fender, 100
FXR, 11, 17, 18, 142–144, 155
Gardner, Bill, 34, 36, 37
GMA brakes, 34, 36, 142
Goodridge hose, 31, 38
Guedes, Jeff, 10
Haak, Dan, 91
Hand, Don, 78–80
Harley-Davidson heads, 92
Harley-Davidson cylinders, 92
Harley-Davidson dresser front fender, 99
Harley-Davidson flywheels, 91
House of Kolor, 23, 115, 124, 126, 132,
    133, 142, 150, 151
HVLP spray gun, 116–118
Hyperformance cylinders, 87, 92
Ignition, 60, 61
Iron Bags custom bags, 135
James, Jesse, 96
JayBrake, 34
Jim's Machine tool, 70
Johnson Performance Engineering cylinder
    heads, 93
Johnson, Alan, 93
Ken's Metal Finishing, 138
Kokesh MC Parts, 32, 45, 78, 153
Koni shocks, 29
Kosmoski, Jon, 9, 115, 118, 119, 126
LaCroix, Jeff, 138–141
Legacy fender, 99
LePera seat, 142
Linscott, Doug, 90, 91
M-C Specialties, 24, 45, 150, 156
Madden, Ken, 132, 133
Martin, Max, 47
McAllister, Mike, 45, 137, 156, 157
McKay, Bob, 136, 149
Merch Performance cases, 87–89
Merch Performance cylinders, 92
Merch Performance heads, 94
Metzeler tires, 47
Mikuni carburetor, 55
Milwaukee Iron, 96
Minneapolis Custom Cycle, 87, 89
Mitchell, Jason, 78, 79
Moon Machine, 17
Mosbeck, Brian, 158
MSO (manufacturers statement of origin), 8
Nybo, Keith, 155
Paint
    coatings, 125
    components of, 118
    custom paint, 119
    Harley-Davidson Custom Paint
    Program, The, 127, 128
    how to, 128, 129
    painting a Road King Conversion,
    130–133
    powder paint, 120–123
    surface preparation, 124, 126, 127
    taping, 129
    types of, 118, 119
Panhead replacement frame, 17
Patrick Racing billet heads, 94
Perewitz frame, 48, 49
Perewitz, Dave, 11, 21, 48, 98, 134, 145
Perewitz/Sullivan Brothers billet wheels, 48,
    49
Performance Machine, 34–36, 38
Petrykowski, Jim, 102, 110–113
Pistons, 92
Polishing, 146, 147

Pro One, 96
Progressive Suspension damper tubes, 28
Progressive Suspension shocks, 29
Progressive Suspension spring kit, 28
Progressive Suspension, 30
Python II exhaust system, 56
Quick Bob fiberglass fender, 98
RevTech cast heads, 93–95
Rivera Engineering billet heads, 94
Rivera SU Carburetor, 54, 55
Road King, 156–159
Roehl, Rob, 102, 105–109, 150, 151
Russell hose, 31, 37, 38
S&S Cycle flywheels, 91
S&S Cycle cases, 91
S&S Cycle cylinder heads, 94
S&S Cycle cylinders 90, 92
S&S Cycle Model E and G shorty carbure-
    tors, 52, 55
Sanders and grinders, 115
Sands, Perry, 35
Scherer, Jerry, 150, 151
Screamin' Eagle camshafts, 57
Screamin' Eagle carburetors, 52, 55
Shallock, Gary, 32, 33
Sheet metal
    chain guard built from scratch,
    110–113
    equipment needed, 101, 103
    fabrication of a simple dash, 106–109
    mounting, 97–99, 101
    welding, 102
Sherwood, Barb, 78
Shovelhead, 46, 53, 136, 137, 142, 143
Siphon/high pressure spray gun, 116, 117
Smith, Donnie, 10, 17, 21, 31, 34, 35, 102,
    103, 106, 108, 134, 135, 150, 153–155
Smith, Greg, 22, 23, 150
Softail, 7, 16, 48, 144, 145, 148
Sportster, 10, 24, 55, 78, 85, 134–136
Spray guns, 116–118
Sputhe cast heads, 95
Sputhe Engineering cases, 91
Sputhe Engineering cylinders, 92
St. Paul Harley-Davidson, 44, 62, 68, 91,
    128
STD cast heads, 94
STD Development Company cases, 90
Storz, 137
Strait, Jaye, 125
Strom, Gary, 45
Sullivan Brothers, 46
Suspension
    changing forks, 26, 27
    front forks, 26
    lowering, 29, 30
    springs and shocks, 27–29
Tank Renew, 155
Teal, Mallard, 115, 118
Tima, Don, 150–155
Truett & Osborn flywheels, 91
Walters competition heads, 87
Wheels
    billet, 40–43
    rim size, 43, 46, 47
    spokes, 44, 45
White Brothers lowering kits, 30
White Brothers, 30
White, Dick, 120–122
Wiseco pistons, 74, 80
Wizard Studios, 159
Wolff, Tim, 62–64, 68–77
Works Performance, 30
X-Drive swingarm, 34